Colorado

Sanctuaries,
Retreats,
and
Sacred Places

Jean Torkelson

Photography by Bill Bonebrake

WESTCLIFFE PUBLISHERS

www.westcliffepublishers.com

International Standard Book Number: 1-56579-390-0

Text copyright: Jean Torkelson, 2001. All rights reserved.
Photography copyright: Bill Bonebrake, 2001. All rights reserved.

Editor: Steve Grinstead
Designer: Angie Lee, Grindstone Graphics, Inc.
Production Manager: Craig Keyzer

Published by:
Westcliffe Publishers, Inc.
P.O. Box 1261
Englewood, CO 80150
www.westcliffepublishers.com

Printed in Hong Kong through: World Print, Ltd.

Library of Congress Cataloging-in-Publication Data
Torkelson, Jean, 1950-
    Colorado's sanctuaries, retreats, and sacred places / by Jean Torkelson;
    photography by Bill Bonebrake.
        p. cm.
    Includes bibliographical references and index.
    ISBN 1-56579-390-0
    1. Sacred space--Colorado Plateau. 2. Colorado--Religion. I. Title.

    BL581.C64 T67 2001
    291.3'5'09788--dc21   2001022520

*For more information about other fine books and calendars from Westcliffe Publishers,
please contact your local bookstore, call us at 1-800-523-3692, write for our free color
catalog, or visit us on the Web at* **www.westcliffepublishers.com.**

*Please Note: Risk is always a factor in backcountry and high-mountain travel. Some
of the activities described in this book can be dangerous, especially when weather is
adverse or unpredictable, and when unforeseen events or conditions create a hazardous
situation. The author has done her best to provide the reader with accurate information,
but it is the responsibility of the users of this guide to learn the necessary skills for safe
backcountry travel and to exercise caution in potentially hazardous areas. The author
and publisher disclaim any liability for injury or other damage caused by backcountry
traveling or performing any other activity described in this book.*

**Cover: The Chapel of St. Catherine of Siena at St. Malo
Religious Retreat and Conference Center in Allenspark.**

Back cover: Salvation Army High Peak Camp in Estes Park.

**Opposite: The Abbey of St. Walburga in Virginia Dale,
a Benedictine community in Colorado since 1935.**

Acknowledgments

This book started with a phone call from a stranger. Linda Doyle, associate publisher at Westcliffe Publishers, wondered whether I, as religion writer for the *Rocky Mountain News,* would be interested in writing a book about spiritual places in Colorado. From there, the project zigzagged its way from possible, to probable, to what you hold in your hands today. At every step, Linda showed me there was fun in this mysterious thing called book publishing. She kept me anchored during the long haul. I thank her.

I'm grateful to managing editor Jenna Samelson for her steady guidance. Like a skilled ship captain, she kept a light hand at the helm during smooth waters and a good grip during the bumps. I also want to thank copy editor Steve Grinstead. At the risk of overheating the metaphor, even landlubbers know one of the trickiest parts of sailing is the last leg—bringing the ship into port. Steve came aboard when the manuscript was done and made it better with his editing and good judgment.

Finally, thank you, Jeanne Walton, for getting this book on paper. Thanks to Jeanne's computer expertise, the hundreds of elements that make up a book were organized into a coherent manuscript. Of course, I never would have discovered Jeanne's talents if I hadn't already been blessed with her friendship. I can't count the number of times she squeezed in a computer session on the way to gymnastics class to cheer on her daughter, Laura. And for all those times during this project when you shared your mother's time with me—thanks, Laura!

This manuscript was nearly done when it hit me—Jeanne and I met on a spiritual retreat. What's more, that retreat center is in this book. I won't tell you which one; I hope the information here helps you find your own special havens of spiritual renewal and trusted friends.

Opposite: The Sangre de Cristo Parish Church in San Luis, site of the famous San Luis Stations of the Cross.

Contents

Regions of Colorado

Opposite: Treasure Mountain
Bible Camp in Marble, near the
Maroon Bells Wilderness.

Regions of Colorado

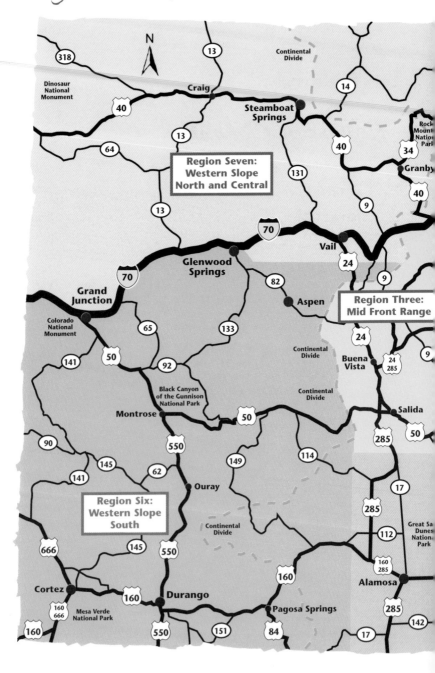

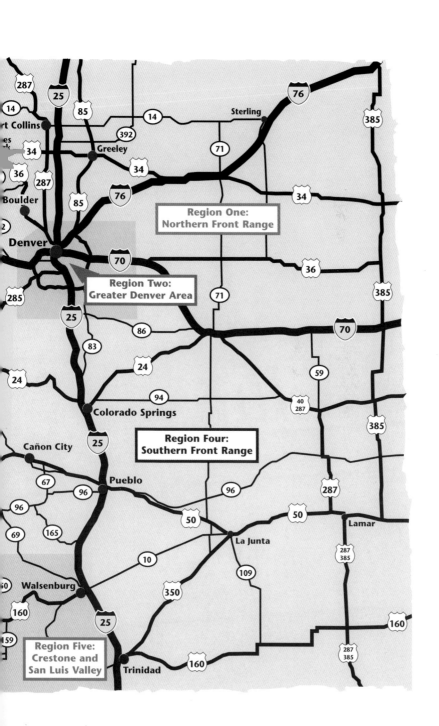

Introduction

A few life revolutions ago, I was in the middle of a career change and feeling harassed when my mother offered a suggestion. "Why don't you go on a retreat?" she said.

What—take time from the résumés? The phone contacts? The quick visit home to the folks?

As it happened (of course, my mother was way ahead of me on this), my parents' church had posted a notice that a prominent spiritual director was to speak at a nearby weekend retreat. An opening was still available. Bemused and a little anxious, I packed my bags and my mother pushed me out the door.

It was just the thing. Spiritually refreshed and mentally refocused, I made good on that lost résumé-weekend—because I realized it had not been a lost résumé-weekend at all. From the moment I arrived at the retreat house I began to recapture the rhythm that existed outside my own little universe. The discipline of a tiny room made it easier to pray. I was eager for some good counsel. As I stepped back from all the "stuff" of existence, it dawned on me that the joys and pressures of life may be significant, but they're not necessarily crucial. They're more like a precious casing around deeper realities.

Sacred places, whether we seek them in an out-of-the-way shrine, an overnight cabin, or on an ancient mountain, give us space to reconnect with those realities.

A lot of us seem to be looking for such places. Fast-forward to a few more life revolutions, when my interest in religion had evolved into writing about it. I began to get calls from people asking, "Do you know of a good overnight retreat place?" Or, "I'm going hiking near Garden of the Gods and I was wondering, is there any religious significance to that?" Or, "I'd like to find a summer camp that would give my child some good religious values, but we're not connected to a church and I don't know where to start." As I and my callers have learned, there aren't many resources to answer those questions. Different religious traditions keep track of their own programs, but they aren't much help with their neighbors' traditions across the street. The Internet offers a delicious smorgasbord, but its morsels are scattered through cyberspace.

The 40-foot-high Tashi Gomang Stupa, a Tibetan Buddhist prayer altar at Karma Thegsum Tashi Gomang in Crestone.

In this book I've tried to draw together answers to all kinds of questions about an array of spiritual traditions throughout Colorado. It doesn't hurt that they sit on some of the most inspiring real estate on the planet, either.

One hot afternoon in the summer of 2000, as my research led me over a bumpy backwoods road from a Bible camp to a Buddhist stupa, something hit me. This project was becoming like a comparative religion course for adventurers. As I researched further back in Denver, I discovered that a pretty campus I often passed by was actually a spiritual retreat house—a sacred place I'd like to visit someday myself.

I hope you find many places to explore here, too.

**Bear Trap Ranch near Colorado Springs is
one of four national training centers for
the InterVarsity Christian Fellowship.**

How To Use This Guide

I would be pleased if you considered this a book you could toss in the back of the car, or thumb to tattered ruin by your bedside table. In other words, that you would whip it out as the spirit moved you—literally.

If you're like I am, sometimes you get a sharp, sudden yearning to find a simple room far away from the drumbeat of life, a simple place to pray. Or maybe you're driving down the Interstate and remember hearing about a nearby shrine. Perhaps you're curious about a religious tradition and wonder if strangers are welcomed. (Most likely, they are.)

There are times when we need an afternoon to stretch the soul, or a long weekend away. Sometimes it feels right to put some spiritual values into that family vacation. Or give your child one summer week to mingle faith and fun.

Regional Designations and Maps

We Coloradans already know this is God's country, so it should be no surprise that our divine geography helped organize these soul-stretching destinations into seven regions. The Continental Divide—the Rocky Mountain ridge that divides rivers into easterly and westerly flow—breaks the state in two, like a ragged eggshell. Everything east of the Divide is commonly known as the Front Range. Everything west is the Western Slope. From there it makes sense to further divide these natural halves into north and south. And as shown on the state map (see pages 8–9), the Western Slope North seemed to feed naturally into the adjacent "Central" stretch we've included with it, which runs parallel to the I-70 corridor from the Blackhawk/Central City area westward to Vail and Beaver Creek.

All seven regions sparkle with their own personality. Greater Denver, for obvious cosmopolitan reasons. The Mid Front Range, physically in the solar plexus of the state, opens out into the majestic Tarryall Mountains and Collegiate Peaks. The Western Slope North and Central offers rugged, pine-scented havens in the state's upper latitudes. Spiritual destinations in the Western Slope South are to be found among both craggy peaks and desert country. Included in the Western Slope South is South Fork, technically east of the Continental Divide but linked both geographically and intuitively to the Western Slope by the San Juan Mountains. The Crestone and San Luis Valley area, blooming with an array of religious heritages, is a spiritual destination becoming known around the world.

Each region defined on the state map makes up its own chapter; every chapter is introduced by a regional profile and an area map showing the numbered site locations. An index of the destinations within each region is also included on these opening pages for easy reference. The numbered listings follow the area map and profile, organized consecutively under the headings of "Sanctuaries," "Retreats," and "Sacred Places." Colored tabs help you to quickly distinguish the seven regions.

Listings

Every entry under the headings of "Sanctuaries" and "Retreats" includes a point-by-point factual summary: the destination's name, address, phone number, and, if applicable, fax number, e-mail address, and website address; its general location; a brief description of the place; a guest profile indicating the place's primary users; the type of spiritual experience visitors could expect to find there; and instructions on how to get there.

Now, a gentle disclaimer on directions. I am amazed how differently natives and newcomers peg "where they are." What locals saw as perfectly valid instructions, such as "turn at the big rock by the fence," I tried to translate into something more understandable to first-time travelers. Copy was sent back to the centers for corrections and clarifications. Some changed the directions back to the original. When they did, I took into account that I had been there only once whereas they, after all, were in the business of getting people to their front door. Usually I went with what they said—but I'll take the blame for any errors.

The retreat entries bear special consideration. Overnight getaways vary considerably in their levels of creature comforts, so check out everything to your own satisfaction before committing to a stay. Some resort-style retreats offer private baths, wall-to-wall carpeting, and homey or hotel-quality bedrooms; even so, some of these posh and homelike retreats may offer only a shared bathroom down the hall.

At the other end of the spectrum you may find bunkbed-style dorm rooms in settings that are more backcountry-cabin than Côte d'Azur. Moreover, many bunk-dorms are tiny. You may find it important to your sanity to find out ahead of time, whether for yourself or for your visiting child, how many are booked to a room. The retreat's name can sometimes provide a clue to what you can expect.

The Chapel at Camp Redcloud, an interdenominational camp southwest of Lake City in the San Juan Mountains.

If the site calls itself a "camp," it's likely to have a rustic, backcountry style, lots of kids during the summer, and an emphasis on physical activity sweetened by a religious program. "Retreat centers" are more likely to be geared toward adult spiritual programs, year-round.

But not necessarily. This may be a good time for the "so-I-can-sleep-nights" disclaimer: Nothing here should be considered an endorsement or the final word on a place. A little further investigation on your part into the particulars of a retreat's guest amenities will greatly increase your chances of contentment.

My heart went out to a warmly hospitable couple who run a spiritual getaway in the deep woods of the Western Slope. They told about a group from California who came to spend a week at the outdoorsy and homespun Bible camp. It turned out the guests had been expecting a posh Aspen-style aerie, with—who knows?—wall-to-wall carpeting and linen napkins. All week long the guests complained. They cast a pall over their fellow guests' visit and hurt the directors' feelings, and these are the kind of folks who would do anything to make guests feel at home.

The lesson learned? "Please tell people these aren't resorts," the camp director pleaded.

Note that, in most cases, you will not find prices here or labels such as "expensive" or "easily affordable." That's because virtually all these centers are run as tax-exempt, nonprofit organizations. When I tried to categorize the intricate pricing and donation systems, the book started to look like a guide to nonprofit bookkeeping. Among the many complexities, some directors run modest programs right at the financial edge, and hope against hope that their guests will be more generous than the stated donation. Others feel obligated to suggest a higher donation to begin with, but would never turn away anybody in need. Some offer spiritual programs a la carte and charge differently for each specific spiritual-direction program. You get the idea. It's impossible to express all the combinations adequately.

Now for the exception to the rule: A few destinations, notably the two YMCA complexes (see pages 36 and 245), have made a fine art of accommodation pricing. It would be avoiding the obvious not to acknowledge the cost system that is so much a part of their glossy brochures.

In all cases, however, use the provided contact information to inquire about rates and program changes.

What Are Sanctuaries, Retreats, and Sacred Places?

In these pages are more than 100 ideas for finding your own spiritual fit. They're divided into three main categories: Sanctuaries are places to visit and leave the same day. Retreats offer overnight stays. Sacred Places pay tribute to Colorado's rich spiritual heritage and offer a natural, outdoors setting for your own meditation. Sites I didn't visit because of time or geographic constraints are listed, along with contact numbers, at the end of most regions under the "Other Spiritual Destinations" heading.

Inevitably, some places fall into more than one category. In other words, they could be used as both "sanctuary"—a place to spend time for part of a day—and an overnight "retreat." I've tried to list them according to their primary function. But call them if you have questions about long or short visits.

Each entry tries to give you an idea of what to expect in terms of silence and surroundings. If you're longing for a weekend of quiet meditation, you may not want to be

Opposite: A stained-glass window at Benet Hill Monastery in Colorado Springs.

located near a roaring freeway—or then again, maybe a private room is more crucial than the neighborhood. In any case, I've tried to alert you to the rhythm of each place: whether, for example, you're expected to join in programs or whether you'll be left alone; whether there's a chapel or temple to escape to; or whether religious services or spiritual direction are available.

Assume in all cases that pets, alcohol, and radios should be left at home. (Kids too, unless they're part of the program.)

Finally, some observations about sacred places. As you'll see, those listings for the most part pay tribute to places that are, or have been, important cultural and spiritual sites to Native Americans. These sites are meditative places of great beauty and spiritual significance. But there's a catch: Native Americans in Colorado oppose popularizing many of their most significant places. More than one archaeologist spoke bitterly of such sites being littered with everything from ritual campfires to "New Age" crystals.

What's more, there is a fundamental difference between the Western European understanding of "sacred," as belonging to a church or shrine, and the Native American understanding that "all places are sacred," as Ute historian Alden Naranjo puts it. In Colorado, a strong, activist network of tribal leaders has enlisted the help of park personnel and archaeologists to discourage folks from "sacred-hunting." So what you'll find in this book are places with public access, but no attempts to pass on insider information about private ceremonial grounds.

I had a sharp exchange with an official at one national park who was furious with me for calling attention to Native American sites by calling them "sacred." "When you call a place sacred," she fumed, "you might as well tell people to beat a path to their door." But national park spokesman Will Morris seemed to understand what I was trying to do. He empathized with my wish to include Colorado's ancient spiritual heritage along with its present offerings. Yet Morris, too, warned that officials will clam up if people ask to be directed to "something sacred."

"If you don't know what's sacred," he said, "we can't tell you."

Perhaps that's as good a motto as any, as you take up this book. May you find what you're searching for.

Opposite: A site sacred to the Utes, Garden of the Gods was an intertribal meeting place and remains an ideal natural retreat.

Region One:
Northern Front Range

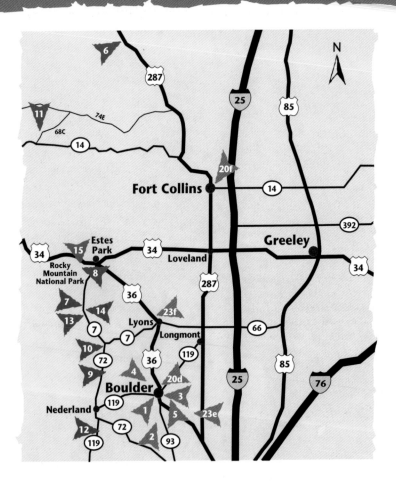

*B*oulder is known as a haven for the unconventional. No surprise it's at the heart of the region with the most eclectic collection of sanctuaries and retreats.

For starters, consider this mix: Hovering near the wildly remote Wyoming border are not one but two major retreat centers. One, the Abbey of St. Walburga, is traditional Catholic, with nuns in long black habits who follow a religious order established 1,500 years ago by St. Benedict. The other, the Rocky Mountain Shambhala Center, is Buddhist, with teacher-monks in the robes and shaven heads of their own 2,500-year-old religious system.

As it happens, Boulder holds the historical keys to both the St. Walburga Abbey and the Shambhala Center. The nuns moved to their hardy, border-town setting from their original home in the city; Shambhala is part of the expanding work of the late Chogyam Trungpa Rinpoche, founder of Naropa University in Boulder, which has become a major center for the growing Eastern influence in American religious life. Naropa is a fully accredited non-sectarian liberal arts university founded on Buddhist principles, offering a wide array of interdenominational master's and bachelor's programs. Naropa's presence undoubtedly has helped make this region a welcoming home to at least four other sanct-uaries dedicated to Eastern religious thought—including another Naropa-affiliated Shambhala Center in the heart of Boulder (see page 22). Naropa also has its own meditation hall (see page 26).

Sanctuaries

Retreats

Sacred Places

Christian camps and centers hold their own in the canyons and wood-lands of Roosevelt National Forest. No fewer than five dot Highway 7, the vista-strewn roadway that takes you from the Boulder area to Estes Park. One such center welcomed a special retreat visitor from Rome—Pope John Paul II, who came to St. Malo's for some R & R while in Denver for World Youth Day 1993.

What will your own favorite spiritual haven be? Will it be the rustic horseback-riding camp, the meandering trails where a pope walked, or a Hindu shrine? Will you find a respite from the world at the far edge of a casino town, or at the quiet center of a suburban cemetery?

Here's a collection of sanctuaries and retreat places for you to explore.

Sanctuaries

1. Boulder Shambhala Meditation Center

1345 Spruce Street
Boulder, CO 80302
303-444-0190

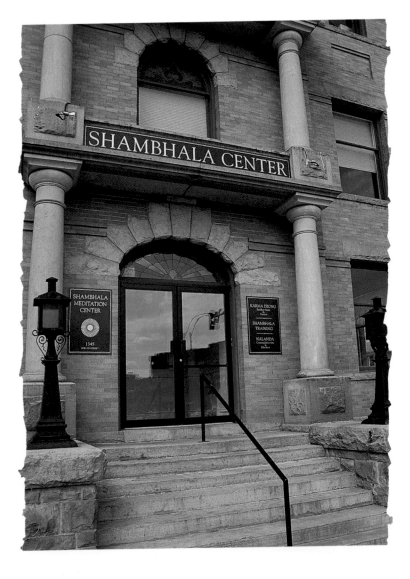

*B*oulder Shambhala Meditation Center, located in the heart of Boulder's downtown residential bustle, is part of the legacy of its prolific founder, the late Chogyam Trungpa Rinpoche. Several blocks southeast is Naropa University, Trungpa Rinpoche's original teaching institute. (For more about Naropa and the Red Feather Lakes Shambhala location, see pages 26 and 42.) Today, Trungpa Rinpoche's programs and teachings are carried on by his son, Sakyong Mipham Rinpoche, as well as other visiting lamas and senior teachers.

Many classes and educational opportunities are offered here in this rambling old Victorian-style building, restored to a cozy, creaky simplicity. There are two meditation halls—one in serene, minimalist style (cushions on the floor, an altar, candles) and the other a visual explosion of glittering golds and reds. Both are used for regular, daily meditation.

Call for the full array of times and events.

Location: One block north of the Pearl Street Mall in central Boulder.

Description: A Buddhist meditation and practice center founded by Chogyam Trungpa Rinpoche.

Guest Profile: All welcome.

Spiritual Experience: Quiet meditation. Education and other programs available.

How to get there: The 1400 block of Spruce is in the center of Boulder, one block north of Pearl. If you come to town from Denver on Highway 36, you'll end up on 28th Street. Take Spruce left (west) to 14th. The center is on the northwest corner of 14th and Spruce.

Opportunities include an introduction to Buddhism on Mondays at 7 p.m. and a Sunday open house at 10:30 a.m. with meditation instruction for newcomers. On weekdays, the center is open for individual meditation from 11 a.m. to 6 p.m. and group meditation Sundays from 9 a.m. to noon and 2 to 5 p.m. In the spirit of Trungpa Rinpoche's breadth of interests, the center also offers programs in contemplative arts and education. These include *kyudo*, or Japanese archery, and *ikebana* flower arranging, the graceful, balletic style recognized as the quintessential "Oriental art."

2. Eldorado Mountain Yoga Ashram

c/o Shambhava School of Yoga
2875 County Road 67
Boulder, CO 80303
303-494-3051
www.eldoradoyoga.org

*T*imes continue to be good for the Eldorado Ashram. From its small beginnings in the early 1980s in a building near the campus of the University of Colorado, the ashram has expanded to 25 acres of prime land beneath the brow of the famous Flatirons. The companion center, with overnight accommodations, is near Nederland (see page 46).

Here, followers of the Hindu yogi, Swami Shambhavananda, have made their year-round home. The swami spends much of his summer at this ashram and the center near Nederland. He's also involved in building related ashrams around the United States, including his newest in Hawaii.

The centerpiece of the grounds is a light, airy temple in a striking, geodesic-dome style. Underneath the temple's construction are mantras—both written out in paint and traced in the drying cement—designed to bring harmony to the environment. As followers explain, the mantras are composed of syllables whose vibration is higher than normal, which they believe lends a meditative quality to the atmosphere. In this setting, followers take up yoga to learn techniques for a richer life. In 2000, the classes included yoga for stress reduction, for beginners, and for those over 40. Another was entitled "Unleashing the Athlete Within." There are also meditation classes and weekend retreats, and advanced classes for yoga teachers.

The public is invited to several free "drop-in" events, including the regular Monday meditation and dinner, which begins at 6 p.m., and the daily "Aratis," or

Location: 5 miles outside of Boulder.

Description: A Hindu daytime spiritual center for learning yoga and using it to lead a richer life.

Guest Profile: Anyone wishing to take yoga classes. You must ask ahead for permission to meditate in the temple. (For overnight and extended retreat stays, see the Shoshoni Yoga Retreat in Nederland, page 46.)

Spiritual Experience: The goal is to attain expertise in Eastern meditative practices and especially yoga, a method for strengthening and relaxing the body and nervous system. Yoga practitioners say it promotes a balanced and expanded state of awareness.

How to get there: Eldorado Springs is just off Highway 93, the "backcountry" route to Boulder from Denver. As you come toward Boulder, stay alert for the Eldorado Springs turnoff, or Highway 170, on the left. It's the last of several major stoplights before you reach Boulder. If you start in Boulder, take Highway 93 (Broadway) south. As you leave town, crossing Table Mesa Drive, you are 2.5 miles from the Eldorado stoplight and turnoff, to your right. Turn right and follow the road 2.5 miles to County Road 67. Turn left at the Yoga Ashram sign. Continue up the dirt road 0.2 mile and turn right into the Ashram property, marked by a sign.

chanting with dancing, every day at 11:30 a.m. The ashram has too small a staff to permit spontaneous arrivals and round-the-clock guests. (In other words, if you come here unannounced, you'll likely find the temple closed.) But during open house times, you're treated to a lovely temple setting, adorned with all the color and glitter of Hindu expression. The eye feasts on a gallery of gods and goddesses, in teak, marble, massive stone, and glittering jewelry, including the elephant-faced god, Ganesh; the blue god, Krishna; the remover of all difficulties, Durga; and Lakshmi, the goddess of wealth and prosperity.

3. Naropa Meditation Hall

2130 Arapahoe Avenue
Boulder, CO 80302-6697
303-546-3572
www.naropa.edu

$\mathcal{T}$he Dalai Lama. Allen Ginsberg. Chogyam Trungpa Rinpoche. These are just some in the gallery of guests and founders who have given Naropa its personality and purpose. The Dalai Lama, spiritual and temporal leader of the Tibetan peoples, visited in the late 1990s. Ginsberg, the Howl poet and icon of the Beat Generation, was an early Naropa supporter and taught here, most famously in the writing and literature program, where he founded the Jack Kerouac School of Disembodied Poetics. And Naropa's founder was Trungpa Rinpoche, a charismatic Buddhist from India whose genius was in knowing how to adapt Eastern spiritual principles to the American way of life. Today there are about 2 million American Buddhists, and some can trace their spiritual home back to Naropa. It was founded on the principles of a sixth-century Indian university once presided over by a great Buddhist scholar named Naropa.

Whether you are a harried student or just swinging through town on an errand, the meditation hall is open to you during the day (usually 9 a.m. to 5 p.m.). The room, perhaps 15 by 20 feet, is by some Buddhist standards very simple. A few blocks away, for example, is the Shambhala Center (see page 22), which glitters with red and gold. It too was founded by Trungpa Rinpoche.

Here, a simple deep blue border frames an altar adorned with flowers, an open Oriental fan, and simple candle-lighting items. Note the rather battered-looking old chair to the right—Trunga Rinpoche sat in that chair when he taught classes here in the '70s and '80s, until his death in 1987. There is nothing stuffy or intimidating about the hall and really only one Buddhist rule of etiquette: You must remove your shoes before entering. If others are already there, that's okay; you're not bothering anybody. Just find a cushion and settle in.

Location: Central Boulder.

Description: A shrine room in the main building of the Naropa University campus.

Guest Profile: Anyone with an interest to meditate in a Buddhist-style shrine hall.

Spiritual Experience: Silence is maintained, though you may well be joined by others also meditating, cross-legged, on prayer cushions.

How to get there: From Denver, take Highway 36 all the way into Boulder, where it becomes 28th Street. Proceed a few blocks north to Arapahoe and turn left (west). Naropa is six blocks down, on the left side of the street. It's a big, deep red brick building that looks like an old-fashioned high school. If no one's at the front desk, walk behind the desk to your right and look for the sign directing you to the shrine.

4. StarHouse

P.O. Box 2180
Boulder, CO 80306
303-245-8452
Fax: 303-443-5375
www.starhouse.org

*A*s you pull up to the parking area, you'll know why this site was selected as a nature-worship experience. Rolling hills frame a visual dessert for the eye, as, far below, shimmering Front Range flatland stretches into the eastern horizon.

Less than a three-minute walk away you'll come upon another arresting sight. StarHouse, the ceremonial center, is architecturally interesting, with subtle, pagoda-like flairs. It was constructed along traditional cathedral and temple lines "as well as ancient geometric

Location: Tucked into Sunshine Canyon about 4 miles from Boulder.

Description: A trans-denominational community, formally called All Seasons Chalice, dedicated to "honoring earth and all beings through ceremony, theater, music and dance."

Guest Profile: Anyone interested in specific events dedicated to season celebrations and ceremony.

Spiritual Experience: Events and classes only; no overnight accommodations.

How to get there: StarHouse accepts no drop-ins. Call for event times. Directions are included on the phone line.

principles of ideal symmetry proportion and harmony," according to spokesperson Laura-Lea Cannon. You'll immediately note the large, Stonehenge-type stones encircling StarHouse. That's exactly what they're meant to represent: Stonehenge, that famously mysterious and ancient circle of stones set in rural England by long-ago practitioners of ancient sun- and nature-worshiping spiritual forms. Like the ancient Stonehenge, "this circle of stones is meant for protection, presence, and grounding," says Cannon.

On this 35-acre expanse, All Seasons Chalice holds events such as solstice and equinox celebrations. The nonprofit group is shifting in 2001 to do more classes and study programs in addition to some public events. The overall belief system tends to ancient nature celebrations, making it a welcoming place for pagans and New Agers, though Cannon cringes at typecasting: "We really struggle with this. We're looking for ways to hold a container of people of all spiritual inclinations."

If you come here on your own, you may see a sign along one of the trails that pleads for silence on behalf of nearby residents. It goes on to say: "Gilbert and Ann White established All Seasons Chalice 40 years ago. We would love to hear about any unusual or interesting phenomena that you experience—animal sightings, wind events, etc."

5. Wall of Life

Sacred Heart of Mary Catholic Church
6739 South Boulder Road
Boulder, CO 80303
303-494-7572
Fax: 303-494-7371

Location: At the edge of a parish cemetery near Boulder.

Description: A shrine dedicated to the unborn.

Guest Profile: Anyone wishing to pause for prayer or meditation, especially those who have suffered the loss of an unborn child.

Spiritual Experience: Solitude, though not necessarily full seclusion: You are near busy South Boulder Road.

How to get there: Take Boulder's Table Mesa Drive—a major east/west street—east (it turns into South Boulder Road when you get to the Highway 36 intersection). Keep going east 2.3 miles. Look for a very big church campus on your left. The cemetery is at its east end.

*T*here are no rules here to follow, no benches to sit on, no ornate building to settle in: just a statue of a majestic yet compassionate Jesus, arms outstretched. The shrine is modeled after a national monument to the unborn in Tennessee. Its full message and significance are a gift meant only for those who stop to pray.

Retreats

6. Abbey of St. Walburga Retreat House

32109 North US Highway 287
Virginia Dale, CO 80536-8942
970-484-1887
www.walburga.org

*J*ust as a young man melts at the mention of his beloved, many veteran retreat-goers melt at the mention of the Sisters of St. Walburga. Everyone who stays here for a spell, no matter what their religious background, seems to fall in love with these cheerfully reserved Benedictine nuns, gracefully clad in long, black habits.

Of course, some people's favorite vision is less formal. You haven't seen anything until you've seen a young Walburga nun striding toward the barn area (off limits to

Location: About 5 miles from the Wyoming state line, about 35 miles equidistant between Laramie and Fort Collins.

Description: A solitude-based retreat experience run by contemplative Catholic nuns who belong to a 1,500-year-old order that follows the Rule of St. Benedict.

Guest Profile: All are welcome to this Catholic retreat house, but guests are asked to observe silence and solitude.

Spiritual Experience: Opportunities for an intensely meditative getaway. Guests may attend daily Mass and join the nuns several times a day for formal prayer. Between the chapel and the wild, rugged terrain are many private opportunities for solitude.

How to get there: From Fort Collins, take Highway 287 (College Avenue) north. (If you're on I-25, take the Laramie/Ault exit, or Highway 14, into Fort Collins. Go 3.3 miles to Riverside Avenue, and veer right onto 287. After a mile, veer right onto College.) Go north about 35 miles over interesting and eerie mesa land. At marker 375 you are 5.8 miles from the left turn to the abbey. When you pass a tiny, white clapboard country church you are a little more than a mile away. The abbey sign is unobtrusive and the turn comes up quickly. You are about half a mile away when you pass the Virginia Dale sign. Watch for the "Point of Interest" sign. The left turn to the abbey is less than 100 feet beyond.

guests), a woolen cap smashed over her flowing veil, a pair of sturdy work jeans peeking out from beneath a billowing, ankle-length, striped work dress.

Here, guests of St. Walburga Abbey get more than a spiritual getaway. They get to look in on the classic life of a Catholic nun in the 21st century. Far from losing its punch in the modern world, the community, which came to the Boulder area in 1935—and to the United States in the mid-19th century—has proved increasingly popular both as an informal retreat getaway and as a monastic community for new generations. So, to expand, the nuns moved to this donated acreage in the late 1990s. Here, on toughened land of gnarled scrub forests and glacier-strewn boulders, this monastic community leads a life of disciplined, regular prayer times and daily work, cloaked in the silence that has been part of the Christian monastic experience for centuries.

But as you'll see, silence here is companionable, not somber. Hospitality has a big role in the Benedictine experience, so even in silence you'll find that hospitality in a quick smile and willingness to point out the coffee maker and kitchen utensils.

This is, in short, a very cheerful place.

Guests are invited to join the nuns at Mass and at the recitation of the Daily Office, the ancient prayers of the Catholic Church, which are prayed and sung seven times a day. Everyone gathers in the wood-beamed chapel, a beautiful destination of skylights and windows—inviting in both sun and moonlight—that offers a glimpse of the rolling hills and canyons that mark this rugged landscape. The altar and golden tabernacle, which contains the Blessed Sacrament, form the focal point of meditation. Overhead is a modern crucifix that an English nun crafted out of the red clay of the Walburga fields.

The chapel and central buildings form the first completed part of a massive building project that will someday include an entire wing for retreatants. Be sure to pick up the literature that details the abbey's architecture and holy items, from its copper-clad dome to the large bronze statue of the patroness of the abbey, St. Walburga, a missionary sister to Germany more than 1,000 years ago. Until the new retreat wing is completed, guests stay in a cluster of comfortable, carpeted modular housing a brisk five-minute walk from the chapel and monastery. There are currently 16 single rooms, simply laid out with bed, chair, and desk. Guests share bathrooms along the hallway. The abbey is closed to the public in January; and even in summer months be sure to bring warm clothing and sturdy hiking shoes—it's a year-round necessity in this rugged area.

As of 2001, food service is limited but that too will change when the new wing is complete. For now, guests are asked to bring their own food. Full kitchen facilities are provided.

So, in a sense, guests are taken up into the rhythm of the sisters themselves—from cooking to praying, from work to hymn singing. While the cloistered monastery is off limits to guests, there are many opportunities to catch glimpses of the nuns going about their work, which ranges from managing farm operations to overseeing the well-stocked gift shop, the computer room, and, indeed, the growing demand for retreat facilities.

7. Covenant Heights Conference Center

7400 Highway 7
Estes Park, CO 80517
970-586-2900
www.covenantheights.org

Location: Under the granite gaze of Mt. Meeker, Longs Peak, and Mt. Lady Washington.

Description: A rough and ready complex affiliated with the Evangelical Covenant Church of America, open to Christian youth and groups.

Guest Profile: Church retreat groups and summer campers from third to twelfth grade.

Spiritual Experience: An interactive, "high adventure" experience with secluded trails available for getaways.

How to get there: From Boulder, take either Highway 36 (28th Street) or Broadway north. Follow the signs to Lyons. In Lyons, the road splits between Highways 36 and 7. Take 7. (Covenant Heights is 24.5 miles from this point.) When you see the sturdy stone church of St. Malo's on your left, you're 2 miles from Covenant Heights. You'll see a sign for Longs Peak Trail, a left turn. Covenant Heights is just beyond that turnoff, to the right.

*W*hat a cheery place for kids. The campus "green" at the center boasts a basketball court, swings, jungle gym, and trails leading out into the great beyond. Beyond is 60 acres of hiking, biking, rock and mountain climbing, and a great little lake engorged with trout. (The policy is catch 'em and throw 'em back.) This camp is home base for Christian Adven-tures, a nationwide outdoor program that serves up its Christian message in a hardy atmosphere. One program leads campers on a three- to four-day backpacking trip into the wilderness—a time of spiritual and physical striving.

There's lodging for anywhere from 15 to 165 guests year-round (15 is the minimum for dining privileges), in frame lodges with bunk beds and shared bath facilities. Whether for kids or for adult Christian groups, the idea is "to build strong new relationships with fellow campers and with God through fun activities, personal Bible study and group chapel sessions."

8. YMCA of the Rockies/ Estes Park Center

2515 Tunnel Road
Estes Park, CO 80511-2550
970-586-3341
www.ymcarockies.org

*Y*ou're looking for a spiritual retreat? Here, the scenery alone is helium for the soul. Your first sight pulling into the grounds is a welcoming committee of towering giants sporting very big shoulders: the massive peaks of Eagle Cliff, Fairchild, Mt. Ypsilon, Bible Point, and Emerald. Spread beneath their high-minded gaze is a wonderful open area, which begs for a guest's early morning walk or run. Even if you don't usually get up at 5 a.m. to work out, you may be tempted to do so here just to see morning break on these mighty granite faces.

Like the peaks, this conference center is done in huge, granddaddy proportions. It can sleep 4,000 people. Dining is all-you-can-eat buffet style. There are so many types of cabins and rates, you really need a brochure to figure out all the players. Here's an example: four-person cabins cost about $60 a night in 2000, while four-bedroom "vacation homes" went for more than $200 a night. Depending on availability, couples and individuals can also rent any of these. The good news is that the rates are flat fees, not per-person rates.

Stringently nondenominational, this nonprofit center is open to any and all. Recent conferences included an evangelical Christian youth rally and an international Buddhist conference. You get the idea.

Location: About 3 miles outside of Estes Park, alongside Rocky Mountain National Park.

Description: A year-round, "full service," 860-acre nonprofit conference and family center with a glossy, professional style—backed by full-color brochures, charts, and graphs listing multiple payment tiers, minimum stays, etc.

Guest Profile: Anybody, individuals to groups. Note: Preference on dates and cabin availability goes first to cabin donors (donor opportunities begin in the five-figure range), and next to those who hold an annual membership to YMCA of the Rockies. (For a family, that came to $150 in 2000.) All others pay a small, one-time guest membership fee.

Spiritual Experience: Exactly what you want to make it. Inspiration provided by nondenominational Sunday services in the chapel, and by Mother Nature everywhere else. A full-time chaplain is available.

How to get there: From the center of Estes Park, follow signs for Highway 36 and the way to the headquarters of Rocky Mountain National Park. After a right turn at a stoplight, drive 1.7 miles along "motel row," a busy tourist highway bristling with nicely kept overnight spots, gas stations, and eateries, and continue straight through a stoplight intersection. A few hundred yards later, look for the sign indicating 66 Road, which veers left. Take this and drive 2 miles, keeping an eye out to your right for the entrance sign to YMCA of the Rockies/Estes Park Center.

9. Glacier View Ranch

8748 Overland Road
Ward, CO 80481
303-459-0771
Fax: 303-459-3325

*I*n 1950 Glacier View Ranch began as a summer camp for kids. That hasn't changed. But today, a handsome lodge and many other amenities have made this 550-acre camp a September-to-May getaway for adults, too, especially pastors' and church groups and spiritual-theme weekends such as marriage encounters.

The overnight accommodations are very comfortable, with 50 motel-style rooms (and private baths) in the main lodge. Kids bunk down in hardier cabins that dot the pretty, boulder-strewn campus. There's a chapel that seats 450, a cozy cafeteria with a stone fireplace, and a wonderful, Junior Olympic–size indoor pool. Unique to Glacier View is an indoor tunnel system that keeps guests cozy as they walk to and from the main buildings. The tunnel is practical indeed. Here, the name Glacier

View really means something: In the winter, at 9,000 feet high, snow and wind are always on the guest list.

Glaciers, of course, often leave behind not just a boulder-strewn landscape but beautiful glacier lakes. You'll find a stunning one here—including a full walk-around of more than a mile. Set high along the lakeside, with a drop-dead view of the toothy peaks, is the property's original log cabin. Leadership teams often choose this quaint, century-old haven, set apart in solitary splendor, as their home base during conferences.

Adult guests bring their own programs and leadership. Seventh Day Adventist staff run the summer programs. The camp observes Saturday Sabbath and laces the activity and entertainment with religious themes such as "a walk through the Bible."

Location: 20 miles west of Boulder.

Description: A year-round Christian retreat and conference center operated by the Rocky Mountain Conference of the Seventh Day Adventists.

Guest Profile: Interdenominational. Youth in the summer; adults, families, groups, and individuals the rest of the year.

Spiritual Experience: Large acreage with inspiring views; offers many chances for solitude, as well as activities from backpacking to skiing, fishing, and horseback riding.

How to get there: In Boulder, going north on Broadway, you will reach a highway intersection with a sign indicating the way to Lyons and Highways 7 and 36. (From Highway 36, follow the signs through town to that intersection.) From there, set your odometer at zero. Drive north about 4.9 miles, past Foothills Park, Neva Road, and Nebo Road. Watch for the sign to Ward/Jamestown. Go left on Lefthand Canyon Drive. After 13 miles you'll drive through the old mining town of Jamestown. (Watch for a wicked speed bump that could rattle your teeth.) At 17.8 miles, the pavement ends. Keep going, and you'll break out into a beautiful welcome mat of meadow stretching off to towering peaks. At 19.1 miles look for the "Glacier View" sign, and drive another 0.4 mile to the lodge.

10. Highlands Presbyterian Camp and Retreat Center

P.O. Box 66
Allenspark, CO 80510
303-747-2888
Fax: 303-747-2889
www.highlandscamp.org

At the turn of the last century, this 285-acre getaway was home to Miss Augusta's summer rental cottages. After World War II the Presbyterian Church bought the property. Today, the camp is an attractive and comfy cluster of handsome cabins—some dating back 100 years—that have been comfortably modernized. All have their own bathroom and shower, and some have stone fireplaces.

The dining hall is as rough-hewn as the cabins are cozy. It's an old World War II barracks hauled here from Greeley that stands about nine feet across. Rumor says it once held German POWs. A multi-million-dollar capital campaign is under way to add to the rustic main facilities and enhance adult retreat opportunities. By the early 2000s there should be a new dining hall and main lodge, which will allow different groups to operate more independently of each other.

Location: Between Boulder and Estes Park.

Description: A summer youth camp and year-round retreat getaway for adults, families, groups, and individuals.

Guest Profile: Groups of all kinds, including youth, church, and nonprofit organizations.

Spiritual Experience: Both interactive and secluded, with trail getaways and cabins often available for individuals or couples.

How to get there: From Boulder, go north on Highway 36 to Lyons. Take Highway 7 left toward Allenspark. Drive another 16 or 17 miles to a sign marked "Business Highway 7." As you draw within a few miles of the camp, start looking for a sign to Peaceful Valley. Beyond it is a scenic pullout and just beyond that, the left turn to Business 7. You will immediately see a huge rock with a big sign for Highlands. That's the dirt road turnoff.

Even now, this is a center with personality. During the summer, kids have horseback riding, mountain bikes, hiking, a challenge course, and, in the back yard, a mountain to climb. That nameless peak, marked by three crosses at the top and towering at about 11,000 feet, has rewarded countless hardy hikers—not just kids—with spectacular sunrises.

There's a lovely outdoor chapel, known as Vespers Site, with a cross of lashed logs and an awesome, in-your-face view of a massive Fourteener, Mt. Meeker. Worshipers attest that the macho massif often greets the rising sun arrayed in a dress of orange, pink, and purple.

The camp encourages a reputation as a retreat center for small groups and individuals. It's worked hard at coming up with some interesting programs, which you're welcome to sign up for as an individual. (Many other retreat centers limit sign-ups to groups only.) The programs here include a grandparent/grandchild camp and a "keenage" camp for those 55 and over. There's a women's faith and fitness program, too, and space for everything from family to pastor retreats.

The camp tries to be especially friendly to those who like to get away by themselves or with a spouse for spiritual renewal. For example, if you sign up for a private cabin, you are guaranteed it will stay private, even if other beds around you go empty. (Obviously during the busy season that may not be possible.) But all else being equal, "we don't bump people," says the office coordinator, the Rev. Lance Loveall.

11. Rocky Mountain Shambhala Center

4921 County Road 68C
Red Feather Lakes, CO 80545-9505
970-881-2184
Fax: 970-881-2909
www.rmsc.shambhala.org

*R*ocky Mountain Shambhala Center is inspired by a tradition: The basis of enlightened society is the understanding that human beings inherently possess wisdom, compassion, and goodness. The center fosters society's well-being by offering individual and group retreats focused on meditation practice and other contemplative disciplines.

Location: A remote backcountry setting about 25 miles from the Wyoming state line and 45 miles from Fort Collins.

Description: A Buddhist center for meditation and education. It's the largest of seven rural retreat centers in Europe and the Americas. In the late 1990s it expanded its facilities to include not just a summer but a year-round retreat program.

Guest Profile: All welcome; tours offered Sundays to day visitors. Call for times.

Spiritual Experience: For those seeking meditation and education in the Eastern spiritual experience. The backcountry setting offers much solitude. Be sure to seek out two special havens a short hike away: One is a magnificent stupa rising 108 feet—the largest in North America. The other is a quiet, meditative Japanese Shinto shrine, as low key and refined as the stupa is awesome.

How to get there: From I-25, take Highway 14 west into Fort Collins. In the city, it becomes College Avenue, which heads north toward Laramie, becoming Highway 287. Drive about 20 miles, and look for a sign indicating the turnoff to Livermore; the junction is marked by The Forks, a large restaurant. Turn left onto Road 74E (Red Feather Lakes Road). Continue 16 miles to a dirt road marked Road 68C. Take a left (you'll see signs for a Boy Scout ranch) and drive 5 miles.

Buddhist by tradition but open to all, the center provides more than 600 acres of rugged land for its seekers and teachers and has drawn instructors and spiritual leaders from around the world. The center also welcomes African shamans, Zen Buddhists, and golfers—yes, golfers—for meditative programs. "Golf is a very meditative game," explains Jeff Waltcher, director of the expansion project. Golf instructors, business leaders, and therapists are among the many who may travel here for an enlightening 18 holes or so.

The Great Stupa of Dharmakaya at the Rocky Mountain Shambhala Center in Red Feather Lakes rises 108 feet from its foundation.

Since the mid-1970s the center has offered camp-style tent facilities for its summer programs. But by the turn of the new century, activity and projects had exploded like fireworks. As of 2001, a new, expanded campus is under way, with space planned for extensive meditation and conference facilities as well as more housing. The classic Shambhala housing is still rugged tent-style, so be sure to call to see what's available. The expanded center will offer a new dining hall and kitchen, a children's center, and even a small spa.

Yet the core focus remains teaching and meditation. On a late summer day in 2000, visitors to this remote, forested haven would have observed a quintessential spiritual moment: a handful of advanced retreatants gathered under a tree, listening earnestly to a Buddhist teacher from India who had traveled here for the summer.

Founded in 1971, the center is the inspiration of Chogyam Trungpa Rinpoche, who created Naropa University in Boulder (see page 26) and is ranked as one of the spiritual innovators of the 20th century. It was his vision that found the way to adapt traditional Buddhist thought to the American way of life, creating a new religious dynamic called American Buddhism. The work of Trungpa Rinpoche, who died in the mid-1980s, is carried on by his son, Sakyong Mipham Rinpoche, who often holds retreats and classes here.

There are family camps and a major children's center, with programs in theater arts, poetry, and writing. A newly built Sacred Hall provides classroom space and a gallery for exquisite Oriental calligraphy and the graceful, Japanese-style artistry known as ikebana (a style familiar in miniature bonsai arrangements and the harmonious zigzag of flowering trees).

Guests, whether long-term or for the day, mustn't miss a visit to the towering stupa that rises up from behind the forest like a Wonderland city hall. Glittering with gold and blazing colors of red, blue, yellow, green, and more, the stupa, three stories high, is actually an abstract representation of a sitting Buddha. Inside, a bronze Buddha stands 13 feet high. Other statue deities glow in golden tranquility in the dim interior light. The ashes of Trungpa Rinpoche repose in a reliquary. The stupa has taken more than a decade to build and is expected to be completed and dedicated in the summer of 2001.

Down another woodland trail is the subtler end of the spiritual-expression spectrum: a Japanese Shinto shrine. The pagoda-shaped, natural wood shelter blends into the forest in elegantly simple lines. A path and meditation area embrace visitors in the stillness.

12. Shoshoni Yoga Retreat

P.O. Box 410
Rollinsville, CO 80474
303-642-0116
www.shoshoni.org

The color brochure invites you to "become new through yoga and meditation retreats and renewals." The ashram—the word refers to a hermitage for yogis—has a vitality about it, as guests lounge on the handsome front deck chatting and waiting for lunch to be announced. The well-planned meals are all vegetarian.

The many shrines include the Buddha Rocks outdoor shrine, which offers a climbing path to spectacular scenery overlooking the Indian Peaks Wilderness Area. Indoor temples are available for traditional fire ceremonies, personal meditation, and chanting.

Yoga means "union," or the practice of using a series of physical postures and breathing exercises to attain a meditative state that leads to self-awareness. Guests may stay as briefly as a day ("yoga and lunch"), or for as long as, say, six months. Accommodations range from a retreat hut with no plumbing to private rooms. There are also dorm-style bunk beds and cabins for two. You may even choose to pitch your own tent.

Among the many activities, guests may sign on for a stretch in the Jacuzzi or a private hike to what's locally known as Rollins Peak. Or they may stay on the grounds for a daily hatha yoga class for easing tension, for pranayama (a technique for discovering breath energy), or perhaps for a comprehensive Siddha-Vaidya Rejuvenation Program for "activating the body's dormant repair mechanism."

If you wander the winding, wooded pathways, you will come upon small and exquisitely turned-out Hindu worship spots such as the Ma Shrine, dedicated to the feminine aspect of the divine. Men and women are asked to dress modestly when entering the shrines. Long dresses are preferred for women. Children are welcome, but their parents must watch them at all times.

Location: 23 miles west of downtown Boulder.

Description: A residential ashram or spiritual retreat center, with overnight stays and daily classes in hatha yoga, meditation, chanting, and pranayama (breathing exercises).

Guest Profile: Anyone seeking a period for rejuvenation and relaxation, with interest in learning more about the Yogic tradition.

Spiritual Experience: Opportunities for solitude in a deep-forest location, "a world apart from hectic daily life."

How to get there: From Boulder, take Canyon Boulevard, which becomes Highway 119 through Boulder Canyon. Set your odometer at zero at the traffic roundabout in Nederland (you're 4.2 miles from the retreat center). Go south on 119. At the intersection of Highways 72 (Peak to Peak Highway) and 119, you are 1.2 miles from the center. When you see the Kelly Dahl campground on your left, you're 0.2 mile from the "Shoshoni" sign, also on your left. The center is a mile up a dirt road.

13. St. Malo Religious Retreat and Conference Center

10758 Highway 7
Allenspark, CO 80510
303-444-5177
Fax: 303-747-2892
www.saintmalo.org

From a mysterious meteor at the start of the century to a pope at the end of it—St. Malo's has quite a history. Although its resort-quality, overnight accommodations are available only to those hooked to a religious group, anyone may stop here during the day to stretch out in the wonderful lodge, browse the gift shop, or stroll the grounds in the footsteps of John Paul II.

In 1993 the pope came here during Denver's World Youth Day. There's a plaque saying so on a rock next to a rough path now named the John Paul II Trail, where the pope strolled to pray the rosary. The trail begins just off the parking lot and extends into a lovely secluded glen and beyond.

Way back in 1916, a Catholic priest named Joe Bosetti could never have guessed he would set in motion a retreat center fit someday for the pope himself. During his days off as an assistant priest at the Cathedral of the Immaculate Conception in Denver, Bosetti was a vigorous mountain climber. One day he was tramping through the area when he saw a fiery meteor soaring through the sky, he later reported. He followed the meteor trail to a massive rock at the foot of Mt. Meeker. Today, that rock is the foundation of the graceful stone church that marks the entrance to St. Malo's.

Now the plot takes a turn worthy of the movie, *The Bells of St. Mary's*. The young priest happened to have witnessed the startling meteor event on the property of a wealthy Catholic lumberman named William McPhee. Convinced that the spectacular cosmic show was a sign from heaven, Bosetti persuaded McPhee to donate the land as a summer camp for choirboys. He later persuaded the equally wealthy Malo family, who were Cathedral parishioners, to build up the property.

After serving for more than 60 years essentially as a boys' camp, in the 1980s St. Malo's was renovated into a posh retreat center for adults. Today, the lodge resembles a high-end complex, with 49 hotel-style bedrooms and a number of meeting rooms. The lobby area boasts a modern, four-sided glass fireplace and a view. One anomaly: for such a splendid place, there is no real place for worship services, save a small chapel on the third floor.

But that brings us back to the stone chapel, located a five-minute walk away. It's officially known as the Chapel of St. Catherine of Siena, a nod to the mother of Mrs. Malo. (Yes, there was a St. Malo, too, a sixth-century Welshman.) Guests, who are welcome to stop in any time of the day, may think they have slipped back into the 13th century. Stone cobbles the floor and altar area. Dim light filters through the stained glass. The walls breathe solitude—until your fellow tourists come in, which happens regularly. Named a historic site, the Chapel on the Rock is a sought-after place for Catholic weddings.

Location: The forested foot of 13,911-foot Mt. Meeker.

Description: A Catholic retreat and conference center available to interdenominational religious groups for overnight, weekend, and longer stays.

Guest Profile: All welcome. Individuals may pause here during the day; only group overnight stays available. Some day activities.

Spiritual Experience: Interactive in a conference setting, but with an array of getaway trails and solitude areas, including the stone chapel.

How to get there: From Boulder, take Broadway or 28th Street north. Either will bring you to the major intersection of Highways 36 and 7. Go north on 36 to Lyons, where 36 and 7 split (you now have 22.9 miles to go). Take the left fork on 7, and start up St. Vrain's Canyon. Slow down when you see the Wild Basin area sign on your left, followed by the Meeker Park Lodge on your right. You are almost at St. Malo's, on the left. You'll know it by its handsome stone church.

14. Wind River Ranch

P.O. Box 3410
Estes Park, CO 80517
970-586-4212 or 1-800-523-4212
www.windriverranch.com

*T*here's nothing quite as lovely as pulling into Wind River Ranch. Your first sight is of a neat crisscross of corrals where horses graze on green pasture under the majestic gray bulk of one of Colorado's most famous Fourteeners, the 14,255-foot-high Longs Peak. You're also in direct range of Estes Cone, an 11,600-foot triangle that can be a fun climb even for armchair mountaineers.

Location: 7 miles from Estes Park, 35 miles from Boulder.

Description: An activity-based Christian camp, closed in winter.

Guest Profile: Families, groups, individuals, small conferences.

Spiritual Experience: Activities, inspirational speakers, prayer, reading, interaction with the Christian staff—and 100 acres of land for spiritual wandering.

How to get there: From Estes Park, take Highway 7 south for 7 miles. Look to your left for the handsome log archway marked "Wind River Ranch." From Denver or Boulder, go to Lyons and the junction of Highways 7 and 36. Take Highway 7, and the ranch is on the right—the last camp before Estes Park, about 26 miles from the Lyons fork.

Horses may play a big role in your Wind River experience: The ranch specializes in horseback riding, and rides and lessons are included in the camp cost. But that's only one in an array of activities ranging from Frisbee tournaments to whitewater rafting, fly fishing, and the pièce de résistance—a 40-foot climbing wall with a 300-foot zipline (think Tarzan zipping through the trees on a rope, but you get a safety harness).

This resort-quality ranch also offers solitude for those who simply want to get away from it all. It's operated by Fireside Ministries, a nondenominational group. The Christian staff puts on a spiritual program featuring inspirational speakers and special activities for kids.

The accommodations are cozy and comfortable, and well justify the cost, which is on the higher end as nonprofit camps go. The cabins feature fireplaces, wood-burning stoves, or separate living rooms. The dining room is charming and rustic, with wagon-wheel "chandeliers" and all the log-cabin coziness you'd hope for in a mountain camp at 9,200 feet.

The family-geared conferences welcome traditional families as well as single parents and individuals. Singles and couples are also welcome to come on their own. It's a strain to think of a downside at Wind River —except, perhaps, that it's not winterized, so the season is limited to warm weather months.

Sacred Places

15. Old Man Mountain

A place of dreams, visions, and ritual offerings, this steep granite cone holds an especially sacred place among Native Americans. Ritual artifacts uncovered along its flanks indicate that since prehistoric times Native Americans have come here "to fast for visions that would bring good fortune and spirit power," says Dr. James B. Benedict, a geologist and archaeologist who has researched and written extensively on Old Man Mountain.

Those interested in learning more about this enduring natural monument should seek out Benedict's highly readable research report, "Old Man Mountain." As Benedict writes, the mountain is revered to this day for its significance as a Native American sacred site for at least 3,000 years. "Over the course of untold generations," Benedict says, "Indians have followed prescribed routes up the mountain to obtain healing power, success in battle or other endeavors, and communication with personal guardian spirits." These journeys are called "vision quests": harrowing personal journeys of four days or more, done without food, clothing, or water, designed to take you to the extremes of your physical, mental, and spiritual limits. See Sacred Passage and the Way of Nature, page 80, for an example of a vision quest program offered with supervised preparation.

For those who would like a less harrowing contact with these ancient, wrinkled flanks—besides, Old Man Mountain sits on private property—there's another way. Find a quiet spot just west of Estes Park, Benedict's 36-page report in hand, and gaze from afar upon this ancient crag.

Both archaeologists and Native Americans are protective of this site and worried that the resurgence of nature religions is turning such sacred places into veritable tourist traps. Working with care and respect, and with the consultation of Native Americans, archaeologists have pieced together a history of this most sacred place. As Benedict tells it, in 1982—one in a series of excavations during the 20th century—researchers found an array of prehistoric artifacts, including potsherds, burned bone, and what could be described as art tools. These items, "found on an isolated rock knob with a panoramic view and exhilarating beauty, gave rise to a new hypothesis that Old Man Mountain was a sacred summit." Five clusters of ritual materials were left in various places along the steep sides. At each of these five sites, it appears, spiritual seekers stopped "to smoke, pray and make offerings while climbing to the summit."

Old Man Mountain is located within a mile of the center of Estes Park. To get there, go to the town's main street, Elkhorn Avenue. Drive out of town to the west, staying on Elkhorn. Follow it a quarter to a half mile, and look for Old Man Mountain on the left side of the road. You should find ample places to pull off and get a good look. For a copy of Benedict's report, write to him care of the Center for Mountain Archaeology, 8297 Overland Road, Ward, CO 80481. The report costs $10 plus postage.

Other Spiritual Destinations

Buckhorn United Methodist Camp

970-484-2508: About 15 miles west of Fort Collins, a year-round camp available to youth, groups, families, and couples. Special outreach to physically, mentally, and emotionally disabled.

Camp Timberline, Estes Park

1207 Longs Peak Road, Estes Park, CO 80517; 970-586-7777 (www.camptimberline.com): A summer camp "reaching and strengthening kids for Christ through sports and mountain adventure."

Salvation Army High Peak Camp

7075 Highway 7, Longs Peak Rt., Estes Park, CO 80517; 970-586-3311: "To seek God and explore His handiwork." This year-round camp for youth, adults, families, and groups offers special outreach to the economically disadvantaged.

Upon the Rock Wilderness Retreats

7437 North 95th Street, Longmont, CO 80501; 303-652-0717: Adventure programs for families and youth. This organization also uses land in southern Colorado.

Next page: Salvation Army High Peak Camp in Estes Park features an antique grist mill.

Region Two:
Greater Denver Area

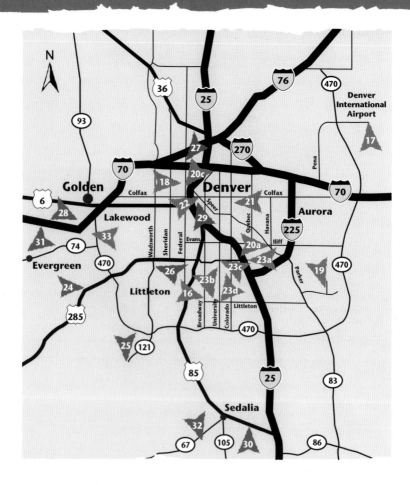

The Denver area isn't just a destination for culture and commerce, but for spiritual sustenance. Following are 18 places where one might go for an afternoon's meditation or a weekend getaway. Or even the last 15 minutes before your flight takes off.

Diversity reigns. Within 20 minutes of downtown Denver, a spiritual seeker could be praying in a hushed Catholic chapel attached to a cloistered monastery, or sitting in a Hare Krishna temple, watching devotees spread petals during an afternoon service. Muslims have three mosques to choose from, including the landmark mosque on Parker Road, which accommodates hundreds—and the first mosque attached to an international airport. And Buddhists may seek out at least three major temples, depending on their lineage.

And geographically? Within an hour of downtown, a retreat experience could be snuggled into a log-bound lodge set deep in a foothills canyon, or in a tidy bedroom at a former convent, perched just off a bustling suburban highway. The interfaith chapel at Denver International Airport is one of the best maintained and most up-to-date in the nation, tended by Christians, Muslims, and Jews. There's even a virtual retreat center of sorts—the place to go to get to some of the best spiritual places in other parts of the state. (Hint: Check out Christ Centered Ministries, a service that offers retreat programs as well as transportation to other destinations around the state.)

Sanctuaries

Retreats

Sacred Places

Sanctuaries

16. Carmelite Monastery

6138 South Gallup Street
Littleton, CO 80120-2702
303-798-4176

Simple. Spare. An afternoon away from the squeezing pressure of work, of chit-chatty radio programs and the ring-a-ling of cell phones. That's what could be yours in just a short visit to the Carmelite Monastery in Littleton. Just off a suburban street is a world unto itself, where guests and worshipers have a place alongside an invisible band of cloistered nuns. You will never see them, but at early morning Mass they are your comrades in

Location: A southern Denver suburb, about 15 miles from downtown.

Description: A chapel and grounds connected to a cloistered nuns' monastery.

Guest Profile: Anyone seeking a spiritual pause during the day. Catholic Mass celebrated Sundays and weekdays.

Spiritual Experience: Solitude in a suburban setting.

How to get there: The monastery is a half mile west of Broadway, a major north/south artery. From Hampden Avenue (Highway 285) drive south on Broadway 2.6 miles to Littleton Boulevard. Turn off onto Littleton. Drive 0.7 mile to Gallup, a side street without any stoplight. Turn left (south), and go a half mile on this park-strewn residential street. On the east side of Gallup you'll pass Ketring Park and the Littleton Historical Society. Gallup Park flanks the west side. Immediately past the Historical Society grounds is the monastery entrance, also on the east side of Gallup Street.

prayer. It is their voices you hear leading the hymns from behind the grille in the lovely, traditional chapel. It's worth noting for its unusual transparent stained glass, statues of Mary and Joseph, and the Blessed Sacrament in a tabernacle directly behind the classic, ornate altar. The grounds feature meandering paths to stroll, and the very pretty Littleton Historic Society grounds are next door to visit.

The Carmelites came to Littleton in 1947. They follow the so-called primitive rule established by their founder, St. Teresa of Avila, in the 16th century. They live in solitude, but they spend their lives praying for the world behind cloistered walls. Their order's name comes from Mt. Carmel in the Holy Land, where the prophet Elias is said to dwell. Though their purpose is not to mingle with guests, they welcome laypeople to their place of rest and reflection. The chapel is open daily for prayer, and they invite you to stroll and meditate on the grounds as if they were your own.

17. Denver International Airport Interfaith Chapel

Denver International Airport
8500 Peña Boulevard
Denver, CO 80249-6340
303-342-2036

*S*ometimes an airport is just an airport—the shortest distance between the security checkpoint and your destination. Other times an airport is a portal for life's joys and miseries—a happy reunion, a time of grief, a place of endings and beginnings. In some of those times, it may be helpful to know a chapel is nearby.

Location: Sixth floor of Denver International Airport.

Description: A nondenominational getaway.

Guest Profile: Anyone seeking a place to meditate quietly or attend regularly scheduled services.

Spiritual Experience: A quiet space in a bustling place.

How to get there: Go to the sixth level of the airport. The chapel is on the southeast side of the main terminal.

When the sky-blue chapel at Denver's high-tech airport opened in 1996, it was done in high style, with representatives of Denver's Catholic, Jewish, and Muslim communities on hand, including a Catholic archbishop and the ambassador of Egypt.

The room itself has 30 chairs and a simple, interdenominational feel. The inset white altar area often has a pretty spray of flowers and little else. An ingenious system allows doors to swing aside for placement of a simple cross or a crucifix. A notable feature, the first in any airport in the country, was the addition of a Muslim masjid, or mosque. Located adjacent to the chapel door, the small, functional masjid is a boon to followers of Islam, including airport workers, who must withdraw from the world several times every day to pray.

The chapel is also available to other denominations for services. A regular Catholic Mass is celebrated on Sundays and communion services take place during the week. All faiths are welcome to use the chapel whenever they wish. It is maintained by an interfaith coalition, who staff it with chaplains available to travelers depending on the time of day.

18. Denver Zen Center

3101 West 31st Avenue
Denver, CO 80211
303-455-1500
Fax: 303-455-1062
members.aol.com/dzcenter

Rigorous meditation, learned over time, marks one as a disciple. But guests are welcome at public sessions on Wednesdays and Sundays. Your education begins when you enter the foyer of this former Christian Science hall. Tucked into alcoves are statue representations of "Bodhisattva." Buddhists revere these beings as exemplifying compassion because they have vowed to liberate other beings before themselves. In the shadowy light, guests may stroll by a graceful porcelain sculpture of the many-handed Kuan-yin, who distributes to those in need, or a faintly smiling Jizo, the patron of travelers, children, and women who have lost children before birth.

Bought in 1998, the center is a work in progress. The meditation hall is bounded by white muslin curtains, with sleeping areas blocked off nearby for members with sleeping bags. The hall itself is complete with

Location: Several miles west, and in full sight of, the downtown Denver skyline.

Description: A meditation center dedicated to a branch of Zen Buddhism hailing from 20th-century Japan. Modern American interpreters were Philip Kapleau, author of *The Three Pillars of Zen*, and Robert Aitken, prolific author whose works include *Taking the Path of Zen*.

Guest Profile: All welcome to a Wednesday meditation session at 6:45 p.m. and to Sunday 9 a.m. talks on Buddhist practice. (Call ahead to confirm.) To participate in longer, more formal meditation and study, establish a relationship with the center by taking out associate or full membership. Introductory seminars on Zen held regularly.

Spiritual Experience: "The center emphasizes sitting meditation as an expression of enlightenment."

How to get there: The center is easily visible from the confluence of Federal and Speer Boulevards and Grove Street. It's the huge, boxy temple-like structure rising up in the middle of this old residential and business area. At the intersection of Federal and Speer, continue west on Speer for about a block. The center is right in front of you.

floor cushions and a serene cherry-wood altar marked by incense and flowers. On special days such as Thanksgiving, members contribute funds and hold food drives to alleviate world hunger. Rising from the center of the altar is a Buddha figure carved in fragrant camphor wood.

As even the uninitiated probably know, the essence of Buddhist thought is the attainment of enlightenment. Buddhists believe that quest of mind, body, and spirit takes a lifetime—and more. The idea is to wrest oneself, while on this earth, from the delusions and attachments that obscure enlightenment. "Our school begins with the idea that all are inherently enlightened," says Shonen Dunley, a priest at the center. "It is our delusions and attachments that prevent us from experiencing it fully. To understand this intellectually or by faith is not enough—it's like having a million dollars in the bank and not knowing the account number. Through meditation and realization, we reclaim what was ours from the beginning."

19. Divine Knowledge Meditation Center

18854 East Ida Avenue
Aurora, CO 80015
303-400-1323
Fax: 303-400-1328
www.divineknowledge.org

*G*uests meet Mondays at the suburban home of Mahatma Rand. If you're shy about arriving at a private home, you might want to call first, suggests Lynn Fonseca, who has studied with Rand for 12 years and helps lead the meditation.

About 15 people attend regularly for two hours of spiritual discourses, meditation, and music. Rand also teaches weekly yoga and meditation classes. As of 2001, classes started at 7 p.m. on Tuesdays at the Aurora Senior Center,

Location: The Denver suburb of Aurora.

Description: Meditation center offering Satsang, a Sanskrit word meaning "being in the company of truth or an enlightened person."

Guest Profile: All welcome.

Spiritual Experience: Guests are taught by Mahatma Rama Nand, who has blended his native Hindu philosophies with Western religions into a universal teaching that promotes "self realization."

How to get there: From the intersection of Parker Road and Orchard, go east 2 miles on Orchard and then one 1 block past Tower Road to Biscayne Street. Turn left. Go one block to Powers, then left on Powers, and take an immediate left on Ida. The house is on the left.

30 Del Mar Circle, and at 7 p.m. on Thursdays at the public library at 14949 East Alameda Drive. (Call to confirm days and times.)

Mahatma Rama Nand arrived from India in 1976. His goal was to spread the "Divine Knowledge of the God Within You." He lives with his wife and kids in Aurora, making his living working in a grocery store while he runs his meditation center. "He's extraordinary," says Fonseca. "I've been with him 12 years, and I've never seen him waver in his dedication and love for God." The Monday night meditation begins with chanted Sanskrit prayers, accompanied by Fonseca on the harmonium and followed by 10 or 15 minutes of silent meditation. Fonseca, and sometimes others in the group, share devotional insights. Finally Nand speaks.

Fonseca explains: "Followers believe that each of us is a child of God, has the divine within us. Those who have come to realize that and living it fully are enlightened beings. That's what Mahatma is."

20. Front Range Islamic Masjids

See locations and phone numbers at the end of this entry.

The Colorado Muslim Society mosque on South Parker Road in Arapahoe County is the largest mosque in Colorado.

*I*slam is one of the fastest growing religions in the United States, and at a growing number of places in Colorado you may practice this 1,500-year-old faith. The mosque on Parker Road in Denver—the largest of many *masjids*, or mosques, in various Front Range cities—is the home of the Colorado Muslim Society. (Consult your phone book for any address changes or new centers.) The mosques are open to the public all day long and into the evening.

At five prescribed times, especially at the noon hour, devout Muslims arrive en masse to say the prayers decreed by the prophet Mohammed. What guests, and even many Muslims, may not know is that every mosque is available for extended retreat periods of several days. Showers and kitchen facilities ensure that spiritual seekers need not leave the building or break their prayerful concentration. This opportunity is open to both men and women. As always, the genders are separated, with women in an upstairs mezzanine prayer room and men in the mosque's main sanctuary below.

There is no cost for this retreat opportunity, says spokesman Muhamed Jodeh of the Colorado Muslim Society.

Masjid locations are listed below. Few attain the huge and majestic proportions of the mosque on Parker. Many are just small rooms, including the masjid at Denver International Airport (see page 60). But large or small, all must face Mecca at the precise degrees latitude and longitude.

Denver
20a. Main mosque, Colorado Muslim Society
2071 South Parker Road, Denver, CO 80231; 303-696-9800.

20b. Denver Islamic Society
2124 S. Birch Street, Denver, CO 80227; 303-759-1985.

20c. Mountain States Islamic Center
2715 Humboldt Street, Denver, CO 80205; 303-296-0948.

Boulder
20d. Boulder Islamic Center
1530 Culver Court, Boulder, CO 80303; 303-444-6345.

Colorado Springs
20e. Colorado Springs Islamic Society
2125 North Chestnut Street, Colorado Springs, CO 80906; 719-632-3364.
(See map on p. 114)

Fort Collins
20f. Islamic Center of Fort Collins
900 Peterson Street, Fort Collins, CO 80524; 970-493-2428. (See map on p. 20)

21. Radha Krishna Temple

1400 Cherry Street (attn: Naikatma, president)
Denver, CO 80220
303-333-5461

*A*irports. Chanting. Head-shorn baby boomers in orange robes. You remember, don't you?

Anyone who lived through the 1970s is sure to remember the early, colorful persona of the Hare Krishna movement. Carrying the legendary seven rupees in his robes, Indian evangelist Srila Prabhupada arrived in New York in the 1960s intent on passing on Krishna consciousness to the West. Young Westerners responded enthusiastically by taking the new religion to street corners and the country's busiest travel centers. Krishna consciousness was raised, indeed.

So, where have all the Krishnas gone?

Gone to temples like this one, and living most quietly, too. Guests are welcome to visit the temple, a former Baptist church sitting on a leafy, residential street alive with briskly moving traffic. Step inside, and bustling Western life drops away. The interior is resplendent with marble columns and parquet flooring. A statue of a seated Prabhupada, looking eerily aware, dominates the room. As you enter the meditative gloom, you may well see devotees seated cross-legged at his feet.

And if you time your visit well, you can indulge in feasts for both the eye and the stomach.

Your visual adventure begins so quietly you may not realize at first what's happening. In the dim light, women in elegant Indian dress glide into the temple at four set times of the day. Curtains part. Before you is a glittering explosion of color: jewel-encrusted marble statues of Sri Krishna and his consort, Sri Radha. The ceremony begins with a boom from a conch shell. A devotee begins to gracefully toss petals and rice.

This is one of the daily ritual offerings to Krishna, whom devotees consider God come to earth, 5,000 years ago. Krishnas begin their first ritual at 4:30 a.m. Visitors are welcome for the rest of the rituals, which, from curtain opening to closing, may take 20 minutes. They begin at 7:20 a.m., at 4:20 p.m., and in the evening at 6:30 and 8:20. (Plan to come at the top of the hour to get the full effect, including the opening conch blast.) The Krishnas also manage Govinda's, a cheerful vegetarian buffet/gift shop open for lunch and dinner. Every Sunday there's a free festival, including food, beginning at 6 p.m.

The low-key hospitality fits with the Krishnas' new persona as members of the neighborhood. The International Krishna Society has bought up a number of homes nearby. And so, in one generation, these exotic converts in orange robes have gone from airport transients to neighbors.

As of 2001, the buffet and gift shop are open Monday through Friday, 11:30 a.m. to 2:30 p.m., and Saturday evenings from 5 to 8. On Sunday, the gift shop is open only at 6:30 p.m., coinciding with the food festival on the grounds.

22. Soka Gakkai International (SGI-USA)

1450 Speer Boulevard
Denver, CO 80204
303-893-0430
Fax: 303-825-7336
www.sgi-usa.org

*T*he breezy entranceway still faintly suggests the former office building this once was. But in the 1990s this setting became home to one of the most successful branches of Buddhism ever to plant itself in the United States. Soka Gakkai took its present form after World War II, as American GIs and émigrés introduced a 20th-century version of the 2,500-year-old

Location: A few blocks from the heart of downtown Denver.

Description: A center affiliated with the American Buddhist Association offering a meditation hall and information on Soka Gakkai, the largest lay Buddhist organization in the United States.

Guest Profile: All welcome.

Spiritual Experience: Guests are welcome to stop by daily for information. (The center is open until 10 p.m. every day but Sunday, when it closes at 6 p.m.) The meditation hall may be open to visitors, based on staff availability. But guests are welcome to come to the daily gathering, usually held at 7 p.m. every evening, when SGI members come together to chant.

How to get there: SGI International is the large, well-marked white building on the corner of Speer and Colfax in downtown Denver. Meter and lot parking is available nearby.

Buddhist belief system. The name Soka Gakkai means "Society for the Creation of Value." In 1930 the Japanese founder, Tsunesaburo Makiguchi, set forth his idea that the purpose of education was to create "value" in society: that is, to work for beauty and the social good.

Today, Soka Gakkai has about 10 million members worldwide and more than a thousand in Colorado. Their Denver center is a multilevel building with a pleasant reception area and rooms for meetings and exhibits. Large gatherings are a hallmark of SGI. The organization is a driving force in the international Earth Charter Project and in big-picture issues such as human rights, environmental protection, and solutions to violence. The Denver chapter also has introduced a Buddhist speakers' bureau.

The meditation hall is laid out in a low-key but reverent style, with simple folding chairs facing a large altar area arrayed in sumptuous gleaming wood. Followers join here to meditate as well as chant their distinctive core phrase, "Nam-Myoho-Renge-Kyo." The phrase represents the essence of the Buddha's teachings and may be translated roughly as "I am devoted to the mystic law of cause and effect."

23. Taize Worship

See locations and phone numbers at the end of this entry.

Calvary Baptist Church of Denver, site of the first organized Taize worship group in Colorado in 1996.

*A*t first sight, this looks simple enough: A congregation has gathered for evening worship. You happen to be among them. But, wait—you don't know anybody here. Nobody knows you. What's more, the person next to you may be Presbyterian or Catholic. You may be Lutheran or Methodist. Or perhaps no denomination at all. Even more unusual, there is no leader, no pastor, no sermon. What draws everyone together is a mysterious camaraderie that transcends faiths, nationality, and even time itself.

Taize worship began after World War II. A group of Protestants and Catholics, exhausted by war, decided to band together to form a monastic community linked by poverty, chastity, and obedience. Their radical new community was in Taize, France. It first spread across western Europe, then to the United States. Denver's first Taize group arrived in 1996.

The evening goes like this: There's usually half an hour of silent meditation, followed by a Scripture reading. Then begins the distinctive Taize chant, a sort of haunting roundelay accompanied by flutes, violins, guitars, and oboes. A beloved variation is ancient Gregorian chant.

Taize has become a global phenomenon, with chants in more than a hundred languages. In a classic—and classical—twist, Latin is the universal tongue in which everybody joins together in unity. Don't worry if you don't know Latin: Hymn lyrics are distributed to the crowd. Or feel free to close your eyes and participate as individually as you choose. (Given the growing number of Taize sites, you may find that each has its own variations.)

Every newcomer is first struck by one thing: How can a random crowd of strangers manage to sound at the first get-go like an award-winning church choir? Nobody knows. But as candles flicker in the darkened sanctuary and voices mount in measured song, people give up wondering how it happens and surrender to a deep peace and unity in solitude.

Many come week after week, and for some it's their only church service. There are no rules, and no mandate to sing. Come and just listen, if you wish. Sometimes the original Taize monks pass through town and lead Bible studies and prayer sessions. But during the Taize service itself, there is no preaching and no pastor, only a leader to keep the music and readings flowing. Silence is the teacher here.

The first Denver Taize group began at Calvary Baptist Church. Today, several Front Range churches have coordinated Taize services.

Location: See below (as of 2001).

Description: A 60- to 90-minute space for quiet, contemplative, Christian-based worship using prayer, chanting, and hymns. A grassroots experience in which the worship rises from the people, not a pastoral leader.

Guest Profile: Anyone who longs to participate in a shared meditative experience with others.

Spiritual Experience: Intensely meditative and very moving: People of every denominational line, and sometimes none, find a common spiritual link in the prayers, hymns, and chants of the ancient Christian Church.

How to get there: All Denver-area sites are easy destinations from anywhere in metro Denver. Two additional sites are in the Northern Front Range area.

Denver

23a. Calvary Baptist Church
6500 Girard Ave. (E. Hampden and Monaco Pkwy.), 303-757-8421.
Worship time: 6:30 p.m., every second Sunday of the month.

23b. First Presbyterian Church
1609 W. Littleton Blvd., 303-798-1389. Worship time: 6:30 p.m., every third Sunday of the month.

23c. Christ Way Community Church
3021 S. University Blvd., 303-758-5664. Worship time: 7 p.m., every fourth Sunday of the month.

23d. St. Andrew United Methodist Church
6325 S. University Blvd., 303-794-2683. Worship time: 6:45 p.m., every fourth Monday of the month.

Louisville

23e. Louisville United Methodist Church
741 Jefferson Ave., 303-666-8812. Worship time: 7 p.m., every first Wednesday of the month.

Lyons

23f. Lyons United Methodist Church
350 Main St., 303-823-6245. Worship time: 7 p.m., every first Wednesday of the month.

Retreats

24. Foss Park Chapel and Conference Center

P.O. Box 684
Indian Hills, CO 80454
303-697-5881
www.fosspark.org

*S*tone-arched and elegantly simple, this chapel is a romantic draw for brides and grooms on their wedding day. The grounds even have a romantic history: They were first developed in 1940 by Martin Foss, a member of the Baptist church, who dedicated his foothills getaway to his late wife. He then bequeathed the lovely setting to the church, which turned the campus into a nondenom-inational conference center complete with overnight accommo-dations for about 40, a fully equipped kitchen, a large dining area, and a cozy fireplace.

Location: In the Rocky Mountain foothills about 20 miles southwest of Denver.

Description: A nondenominational campus for weddings, memorial services, parties, reunions, and conferences. Owned and operated by the First Baptist Church of Denver.

Guest Profile: All welcome. Shown by appointment only.

Spiritual Experience: Geared to events and groups.

How to get there: On Highway 285 (Hampden Avenue), go south from the C-470 junction about 4 miles to the Parmalee Gulch/Indian Hills turnoff. Take that exit, and drive 2 miles or so on the Parmalee Gulch Road. Look for the Foss Park Chapel sign on the left. Continue to a road marked Aztec, and take Aztec about a half mile.

25. Jesus Our Hope Hermitage

10519 South Deer Creek Road
Littleton, CO 80127
303-697-7539

$\mathcal{T}$he 1960s was over, but its powerful backdraft was making Rev. Roger Mollison increasingly concerned. The years following that chaotic time had produced a generation that seemed lost, searching, and disconnected from serious values. In 1983, Mollison, by then a pastor at a Catholic church in

Location: In a winding canyon tucked in the foothills of the Rocky Mountains, about 25 miles from downtown Denver.

Description: An overnight spirituality center set deep in forested backcountry.

Guest Profile: All welcome who are prepared to observe silence, contemplation, and serious rules to protect the environment. (For example, the ever-present fire danger means guests are not allowed to use candles in the small hermitages—only flashlights.)

Spiritual Experience: Solitude is both encouraged and expected.

How to get there: In Lakewood, go south on Kipling Avenue to Ute Avenue. (From C-470, exit at Kipling and go south to Ute, the next right turn.) Go a mile on Ute; follow the curve to the right onto Deer Creek Canyon Road. Go 5.4 miles to South Deer Creek Road, marked by a small street sign on the left. Take South Deer Creek 0.8 mile. Slow down and watch for a hidden entrance sign. Just a few feet beyond the sign is a very narrow dirt road, bounded by a rock wall on one side and a wood fence on the other. That's Blue Jay Gulch Road. (If you get to the fire station, you've gone too far.) Drive about a mile up Blue Jay Gulch, which is extremely bumpy, narrow, and steep. The road will fork; veer to the right. Follow the signs to the "Consecrated Grounds."

Loveland, had enlisted the help of a few fellow investors and decided to establish a place, away from urban complexities, where people could reconnect with their spiritual resources and center themselves.

So began a long and winding road to Jesus Our Hope Hermitage. Set in a thickly wooded area of backcountry nestled high in a canyon along the Front Range, the hermitage now has resort-quality accommodations and a mature and still unfolding mission as an interdenominational haven. Most likely, though, it's still ministering to its original target: the baby-boomer generation now grown up. More than ever, they may be attuned to the spoken and unspoken motto of this place, taken from Scripture: "Be still and know that I am God."

Guests arrive at Clare House, the first log cabin along a rugged upward trail. This is the office and home to the Sisters of Loretto, who now run the center. Farther up the winding trail are the guest accommodations. At the very top are four solo hermitages known as "poustinias," a Russian word meaning "desert." Set at about 7,200 feet altitude, at least a mile higher up than the main grounds, these poustinias are simple wooden cabins—sometimes called prayer shelters—with room for just a cot, stove, and chair. Nearby toilet facilities are outdoors, but a definite step up from outhouses—they're connected to a septic tank system.

The poustinias are named and based on the concept presented in the book *Poustinia*, by Catherine de Hueck Doherty. A social justice activist and modern-thinking Catholic whose work has influenced spiritual seekers since the mid-20th century, Doherty urged that people get away from worldly pressures to find their spiritual center. She wrote that poustinias "are a quiet and lonely place that people wish to enter, to find God who dwells within them."

Between the office and the poustinias along this steep mountain acreage is Francis House,

The chapel in Francis House at Jesus Our Hope Hermitage, a cozy retreat emphasizing solitude and contemplation and run by the Sisters of Loretto.

where most visitors choose to stay. This lovely lodge sleeps about eight in very classy surroundings, in a setting that has touches of a posh hotel. (You may inadvertently break the solitude with a few gasps when you see the sleek modern bathroom in the upstairs loft.) The living area has a cozy gas fireplace and modern kitchen. Downstairs is another elegantly cozy bedroom and a chapel whose windows open onto a natural rock garden.

In keeping with the commitment to stay focused on solitude, the sisters rent Francis House out to only one group or individual at a time—even if it means some rooms go empty. It's felt that throwing strangers together could easily disrupt the quiet harmony of the place. (Individuals or small groups who stay in Francis House might keep in mind that the hermitage is run on a donation basis—so their generosity is most appreciated.)

Now, a final twist to the story.

Slowed by poor health, Mollison has had to watch his inspiration unfold from afar. But little did he know, until years later, that a generous gesture he made more than 30 years ago as a young man would lead to the success the hermitage enjoys today. When he entered the priesthood in May 1964, Mollison had turned over his small nest egg to his parents to enjoy (even though, because he was a diocesan priest, there was no vow of poverty to keep him from using the money himself). Life went on. Mollison found investors to help him buy the original property, including a mortgage, and establish a modest retreat haven.

In the late 1980s, he hoped to expand the property and add some modern facilities. But to do that he needed $85,000, which he simply didn't have. Just about that time his last surviving parent, his mother, passed away. The priest received word of a family inheritance, part of it earmarked for him. Instead of spending his gift, Mollison's parents had invested it for their son's future use. The amount coming to him? $85,000.

26. Loretto Spirituality Center

4000 South Wadsworth Boulevard
Littleton, CO 80123
303-986-1541
Fax: 303-986-8453

The rock 'n rolling 1960s were dicey ground for seeding religious vocations. But it's one of those spiritual ironies that the poor religious soil of the '60s would produce a harvest of retreat centers by the turn of this new century. The Loretto Center is an example. It's one in a class of Catholic centers originally built to train and house hordes of future sisters. But that traditional world was already fading by 1964, the year the Sisters of Loretto opened this 100-capacity novitiate—a convent for student nuns—on a high hill overlooking suburban Denver. The '60s timing left the order with 100 acres of meditative grounds and a building that bristled with empty, one-person bedrooms.

The perfect retreat center.

By 2000, the sisters had already welcomed 8,000 retreatants in just seven years. It was only in that span, since 1993, that the sisters decided to go full-time into the retreat business. Before then, and into the present day, it's been home for the sisters themselves as well as a school for exceptional children. The order was founded in 1812 in Kentucky, where the motherhouse is still located.

In the early '60s, the Denver-based branch was looking for a high hill to place its novitiate. It found a lofty dome overlooking a valley about 10 miles from downtown. Today the scene is an appealing, bird's-eye

Location: A southern suburb of Denver, about 12 miles from downtown.

Description: A retreat center/nuns' motherhouse, located on rolling grounds.

Guest Profile: Anyone seeking a spiritual getaway, in groups or singly.

Spiritual Experience: What you make it: Chapel and grounds encourage solitude, while the location (near a bustling suburban thoroughfare) offers other kinds of getaways.

How to get there: Wadsworth is a major north/south street cutting through the western suburbs. The entrance to the center is on the east side of Wadsworth, just 0.8 mile south of Hampden Avenue (Highway 285).

view of a bustling suburban corridor of restaurants, retail shops, and neighborhoods, framed by lovely grounds. The center's central location and the easygoing accommodations have attracted guests from across the country and a number of religious traditions.

Guests have access to about two dozen rooms. Comfy and carpeted, the rooms are just big enough for a twin bed, a table for writing, a recliner, and a half bath. (Showers are down the hall. A few rooms have full baths.) When the guest list includes men, they get the full-bath rooms so that women can use the shower areas unrestricted. A major renovation project is spiffing up the place, as well as the heating and air-conditioning system. A new gift shop and bookstore should also be in place. Even with the updates, there's a retro '60s feel to the center's long, low-slung corridors, vintage furniture, and walls painted in pearly pink, a color that appears throughout the chapel, dining room, and large meeting areas.

From virtually every window guests are treated to the sight of lush greenery and grounds. Nearby is a small, meditative body of water called Marston Lake. To the west is the stunning view of the Rocky Mountains' Front Range.

The spiritual culture is easygoing. Groups may bring their own retreat director or use the time for their own spiritual questing. The simple chapel features the Blessed Sacrament in the tabernacle, cushioned benches on carpet, and a striking, modern wall rendering of the Stations of the Cross. Here, daily Mass is offered—though not on Sunday, the sisters note with cheerful irony. Sister Mary Ken, who coordinates the retreat center operations, is available for group spiritual direction depending on time and circumstance. Massage therapy and therapeutic touch are offered if an expert is available.

The sisters are among the country's more progressive orders, with a strong feminist and social justice perspective. They welcome retreatants of every denomination or none. Groups range from teachers of inner-city kids to feminist organizations such as Women Space/Women Time.

27. Marycrest Retreat and Conference Center

2851 West 52nd Avenue
Denver, CO 80221-1259
303-458-6270
Fax: 303-433-5865
www.marycrest.org

*D*o you need a few days, or maybe up to eight days, of quiet reflection? Or perhaps spiritual direction for just an hour? The spectrum is open to you at Marycrest. The bonds of everyday stress may start to snap as soon as you arrive at the 26-acre grounds. Your first sight is of a relaxing expanse of lawn and trees meandering up to the handsome complex.

Guests, up to 26 at a time, stay in classic small bedrooms fitted with bed, table, and sink. In monastery lingo they're often called "cells," but the word hardly does justice to these cozy little rooms. Groups should appreciate the four large meeting rooms, including a library embraced by bookshelves. All the rooms are suitable for religious conferences and spiritual groups. The chapel is open for personal prayer. At one end is a quiet area reserved for the Blessed Sacrament. Daily Mass is celebrated in the chapel.

Sister Mary Joy Peter, who runs the retreat house, is one of several sisters on staff who offer spiritual direction. Her credentials include a master's degree in theology and certificates in spiritual and retreat direction. She specializes in helping those suffering from loss, unforgiveness, and life changes. She also does workshops on angels. Other sisters specialize in Scripture understanding, group and couple retreats, recovery counseling, and expertise on "diverse perspectives [spanning] ages, lifestyles, cultures, and personal God-given dreams."

The dining hall—including a smaller room for those who wish to dine separately, or in solitude—is cheerful and serviceable. A coffee pot is always perking and the refrigerator is stocked with everything from cereal to fruit.

The center is run by the Sisters of St. Francis, an international order that began in Holland. The hallways are alive with cheerful artistic contributions by fellow sisters around the world: African madonnas, exquisite paintings rendered on burlap, and lovely oils. The bishop of Chiapas, Mexico, recently stayed on the grounds, and his presence is commemorated in a beautiful and skillful painting.

Marycrest's artistry comes from within, too. Sister Regina paints lovely cards, which are available for sale. Be sure to ask to see the exquisite dioramas and miniatures by Thu Ha, a young Vietnamese woman who is staying at Marycrest while she recovers from surgery. To pass the time, she created a tiny world of the Orient, alive with rivers splashing over rocks, gracefully arched trees, and handsome pagodas. And be sure to browse the wonderful small museum that chronicles old convent life—including a table setting, a cabinet of rosaries and prayer books, and a sequence of doll-models meticulously dressed in the bygone nuns' habits.

The Marycrest grounds bustle with outreach programs, including a food and clothing bank and a job-training center. There's an assisted living complex for the elderly and an assisted living complex for non-elderly with disabilities—believed to be one of the first in the nation. The grounds offer a safe house for abused women and children, and housing for up to two homeless families.

Location: A few miles from downtown in residential northwest Denver.

Description: A center that welcomes guests to "an oasis in the midst of the city" for retreats from one to eight days.

Guest Profile: "Persons of all faiths and cultures."

Spiritual Experience: Solitude or spiritual direction available. Guests are offered "solace from the stress of everyday life and a place to deepen their spirituality in an atmosphere of peace and support."

How to get there: The grounds begin at the corner of Federal Boulevard and 52nd Avenue, 0.5 mile north of I-70. Easy access by driving north on Federal.

28. Mother Cabrini Shrine

20189 Cabrini Boulevard
Golden, CO 80401
303-526-0758

This wild perch, set on the crest of the Rocky Mountain foothills, was founded in honor of the first American citizen to be canonized a saint of the Catholic Church. Sister Francis Xavier Cabrini immigrated to the United States from Italy in 1889, bringing six fellow nuns with her. Ringing in her ears, most likely, was the charge of her Italian bishop, whom she had asked for advice on finding a good group of missionary nuns to join. He is reputed to have said: "I don't know of an institute of missionary sisters. Why don't you found one yourself?"

Cabrini crisscrossed her new country, burdened by a notably thick Italian accent and a burning love for God. She stopped in Colorado, founding one of her many homes for orphans, who always held a special place in her heart. All in all, Cabrini crossed the ocean 24 times and established 67 schools, hospitals, orphanages, and an early version of day care centers across the country.

In Denver, she inspired the hilltop shrine that today is arguably the best known and most popular of any in the metro area, no matter what one's faith happens to be. The only access is up a steep mountainside on a dirt-road switchback. Lift your eyes off the road to take in the Front Range far below, including downtown Denver, rendered in miniature.

Ahead of you is the shrine's most striking feature, visible from miles away: a 22-foot statue of Jesus Christ. The 373 steps leading up to it wind past the Stations of the Cross. The 14 individual shrines commemorate Christ's walk to Calvary. The grounds themselves consist of a cozy cluster of buildings scattered along a hilly, winding roadway. It looks something like a meandering farm. The main building at the far end, which houses the chapel, meeting rooms, and small gift shop, is home to Cabrini's order of nuns, the Missionary Sisters of the Sacred Heart of Jesus. It also has a number of individual guest rooms.

Masses are held in the chapel every Sunday and attract a loyal Denver-area following. Locals have also made the shrine a highly popular—and often crowded—overnight retreat center. A brisk five-minute walk away is a charming old stone house, which also has retreat rooms, most of them dormitory style. Your best chance of finding a room here is to be part of a group.

It's no doubt fitting that this shrine is such a homespun staple in the Denver area, among people of all faiths. After all, Mother Cabrini was a hardworking, no-nonsense nun who devoted her life to reality—helping orphaned kids with nowhere to go. She died in Chicago in 1917 and was canonized a saint in 1946.

Location: In the foothills about 20 miles west of Denver.

Description: A shrine dedicated to a Catholic saint, with chapel, overnight accommodations, small gift shop, and meditative getaways for daily guests, including a Stations of the Cross set on a steep hill.

Guest Profile: All welcome. Mass celebrated Sundays at 7:30 and 11 a.m.

Spiritual Experience: Solitude is easy on this rugged, towering hillside.

How to get there: The shrine is well-marked on both sides of I-70 about 20 miles west of Denver, and 3 miles west of C-470. From either direction, drive about 1.5 miles along a frontage road, watching for the small sign indicating the Cabrini turnoff. (It's 0.2 mile shorter if you're heading east.) Drive 1 mile up a switchback to the "Welcome" sign, and another quarter mile to the main building.

29. Order of Christ Centered Ministries

740–750 Clarkson Street
Denver, CO 80218-3204
303-832-7309 (phone and fax)
E-mail: occminc@earthlink.net

This retreat center offers a moveable feast. The Rev. David Forbes Morgan, an Episcopal priest, has spent decades arranging spiritual getaways throughout the state. Home base for Morgan and his wife, Delores, is two side-by-side turn-of-the-century Victorian mansions in downtown Denver. They welcome small spiritual groups for a traditional Anglican Eucharist service at 6 a.m. Mondays at the Priory House (740 Clarkson); centering prayer follows next door at the House of St. Benedict.

Location: About 1 mile southeast of downtown Denver; various retreat centers located across Colorado.

Description: A religious community holding a regular worship services, providing group meditation, hosting regular retreats, and fostering times of enrichment.

Guest Profile: Any who seek a group retreat experience in a variety of locations.

Spiritual Experience: Group meditation and interaction on a spiritual plane.

How to get there: Headquarters is less than a mile southeast of downtown Denver. Guests usually find their own way to retreat locations, but leaders may arrange pool rides if needed.

A full-fledged "Christ centered" retreat experience is more likely to find you 180 miles away at the Benedictine monastery in Snowmass (see page 221), as Morgan is a friend of the Rev. Thomas Keating, a developer of the popular Christian meditation method called centering prayer. Morgan's retreats most often include teaching that method, which involves learning ways to get in touch with the interior divine essence. Adherents master spiritual discipline by deepening their meditation, using a sacred word (not to be confused with a mantra, they say, which has its own interior meaning).

Other favorite getaways for Morgan and his groups are the Sacred Heart Jesuit Retreat House in Sedalia (see page 89), the Whitewater community near Grand Junction (see page 228), and the Abbey of St. Walburga Retreat House in Virginia Dale (see page 31).

Morgan came by his retreat experience in a Renaissance-man sort of way. He studied chiropractic before joining the ministry, then became president of College of the Rockies, an interdenominational Biblical arts institution no longer in operation. A longing to be part of a more traditional, centuries-old "historic church" led him to the Episcopalians, although his long association with the Benedictines, Jesuits, and other Catholic retreat masters has made him feel connected to that aspect of the Catholic faith.

If you take a Christ Centered retreat, you may be part of a group as large as 60 or as few as 23 (the usual number for a Snowmass weekend). While centering prayer gives structure to the event, Morgan practices a relaxed kind of get-together, inspired in part by his appreciation for Taize worship (see page 72). To prepare for the Snowmass weekends, Morgan asks that everybody get into the Benedictine spirit by preparing a common meal. Guests bring food and wine and settle in for three days of prayer, fellowship, teaching, and relaxation.

30. Sacred Heart Jesuit Retreat House

P.O. Box 185
Sedalia, CO 80135
303-688-4198
Fax: 303-688-9633
www.gabrielmedia.org/shjrh

*W*elcome to a classic retreat house. The longing to pray and meditate may begin as soon as you start up the walk to this graceful, abbey-style building with a chapel rising at one end. Once inside, you are immediately enveloped in a cozy, clubby lodge with a massive stone fireplace and people curled up in comfy chairs under mellow reading lamps. Bookcases line the wall, giving things the feel of a library in an old English country house. Then and there you may decide to extend your weekend retreat to, oh, a month or so.

Something else may immediately strike you: the silence. Not much in life is guaranteed, but you're pretty sure to be in quiet company here.

Location: About 2 miles south of Sedalia, 25 miles south of Denver.

Description: A place of religious retreat and renewal featuring private rooms and an atmosphere of solitude.

Guest Profile: Geared to Catholics, though people and groups of all denominations who seek a serious time of contemplative and prayer-filled quiet are welcome.

Spiritual Experience: Solitude and silence for individuals on private retreat. Group conferences and one-on-one spiritual direction also available.

How to get there: From Denver, go south on I-25 to the Happy Canyon exit (187). Go west to Highway 85, turn right, and continue 3 miles to Sedalia, which is marked by the intersection of Highway 67 and a stoplight. Turn right, drive about 1.5 miles through town, and watch for a sign on the right alerting you that the Jesuit retreat center is 500 feet away. Turn right into the long, winding driveway. If you're heading from the Colorado Springs area, you can exit I-25 at the Highway 85 and Littleton/Sedalia exit. At the stoplight past the outlet center on your right, take 85 north and go 5 miles to Sedalia. From some areas of Denver, it's easier to go south on Santa Fe Drive, which becomes Highway 85.

Groups and conferences may add their own buzz—and music is often piped in during mealtimes—but the general goal is to keep this a meditative, reflective, prayer-filled experience.

At your disposal are 280 acres of rolling countryside, with a mile of walkways on the complex green, including a Stations of the Cross, and several miles of wild and undeveloped trails around the perimeter. A short hike takes you about a half mile off the grounds to a lovely gazebo, which overlooks a postcard-pretty view of mountains and rough-hewn meadows.

For the solitary ambience, you can thank a spiritual tradition that goes back centuries to the Desert Fathers, that group of early religious leaders who contributed to the theology and spiritual practices of Christianity in the church's first centuries. Their instinct for solitude and hermitage in the desert became a hallmark of Catholic and Orthodox meditative experiences, reinforced by medieval monastic traditions. Today, the instinct to seek God in solitude is a cornerstone of the classic Christian retreat.

In the same spirit, guests nestle into a small, one-person room complete with bed, dresser, table, chair, and sink. The old monastic word is "cell," but you will likely find the accommodations quite cheery and cozy. Bathrooms are down the hall. Since you stay in the main lodge, it's easy to pad down at all hours to a cozy stay before the fireplace, or farther down the hall to the small Gothic-style chapel. There, stone walls envelop a classic sanctuary area containing the Blessed Sacrament in the tabernacle. Modern-style chairs surround an adjacent contemporary altar, where Mass is offered daily.

The Jesuit order (officially the Society of Jesus) runs the retreat house and offers a number of "directed retreats" for those who wish to take advantage of them. Priests, nuns, and interdenominational, spiritually trained guides offer programs throughout the year. Call or write for the latest brochure. The center also offers an unusual retreat experience in the month-long "Spiritual Exercises of St. Ignatius," developed by the founder of the Jesuit order 500 years ago. Developed for himself and his followers, St. Ignatius' method of seeking God is now popular with laypeople as well, and appreciated as a trusted way to reach a deeper level of spiritual conversion "turned more completely to God...through the contemplation of Jesus in the Gospels." While a simple weekend stay is on a suggested-donation basis, the 30-day Ignatian retreat ran $1,400 in 2000, including meals and lodging.

31. Transfiguration Retreat Center

(Formerly St. Raphael's Retreat Center)
P.O. Box 1630
Evergreen, CO 80437
303-674-8395
Fax: 303-674-1793

*R*unning a retreat house: That's been Jay and Barbara Valusek's dream ever since they met at one in Texas. Barbara was a spiritual director and massage therapist on staff. Jay, a freelance writer and adult Christian educator, was a guest. They both gravitated to retreats of the silent, contemplative kind, and as a couple they felt it natural to begin a contemplative ministry together. Meanwhile, in Colorado it was the late 1990s, and St. Raphael's Retreat House in Evergreen was in transition. The longtime directors were ready to retire, and the folks at the adjacent Church of the Transfiguration were wondering what to do with their lovely rustic buildings overlooking a rushing brook in the heart of town. They hoped to preserve the retreat legacy synonymous for years with St. Raphael's name.

Fate was about to answer both the church's quandary and the Valuseks' dream.

The couple set destiny in motion by moving with their three kids to Colorado (another life dream), where they began musing in earnest about

Location: In the heart of Evergreen, about 30 miles from Denver.

Description: "An ecumenical, silent retreat center based in the Christian contemplative tradition." (The center has undergone a leadership change and renovation project and expects to reopen in 2001.)

Guest Profile: All welcome.

Spiritual Experience: For individual retreatants, solitude and silence is the norm. The center offers a "sacred space in which to open oneself to God, in solitude and in community." Contemplative prayer retreats offered monthly.

How to get there: Take I-70 to the Evergreen exit (Highway 74). Drive about 8.5 miles past the outskirts of Evergreen and into town, where you'll find the retreat center on your right (on the grounds of Transfiguration Episcopal Church). You're within a mile when you pass a lovely lake on the edge of the town center. Look for a "Meadow Drive" street sign and the gas station/auto shop on the left; the entrance is virtually across the street. If you get to Kittredge, you've gone too far.

opening their own retreat center. Thanks to contacts in a national contemplative-prayer organization, the Shalem Institute for Spiritual Formation, they learned about opportunities at St. Raphael's. This was the chance they'd been waiting for: to create an ecumenical center based on the tradition of Christian contemplation.

The couple arrived in Evergreen in 2000; they hope to have the expanded and renamed Transfiguration Retreat Center open in spring 2001. They plan to make the accommodations cozy but simple: 14 rooms, most of them singles, simply laid out with bed and dresser and with a bath down the hall. Capacity will be about 18 with a few double rooms included. For the truly solitary contemplative, there will also be a small hermitage above the chapel, complete with full kitchen and bath. The name "St. Raphael's" will be memorialized as the name of the center's main guest house.

At least for the time being, guests should expect to bring their own food and plan to use the kitchen. Those who don't wish to mix cooking and contemplation will be glad to know the town of Evergreen is no slouch when it comes to restaurants. Guests may come here as individuals on their own private retreat, take advantage of the Valuseks' monthly retreats, or reserve the center for their own group. Barbara offers spiritual direction and massage therapy, which she says is done prayerfully and blends well with the contemplative spirit they are fostering. There's also a chapel for meditation, and Sunday worship as close as the nearby Church of the Transfiguration.

Groups, as well as individuals, should be ready to plunge into the experience of contemplative silence. As Jay puts it, "We think silence is the greatest gift we have to offer here."

32. Woodbine Ranch

2584 North Highway 67
Sedalia, CO 80135
303-688-3422
Fax: 303-688-8998
www.woodbine.org

It used to be a honky-tonk with a gambling den in back. When Woodbine Ranch took over in the 1950s, it kept the rollicking, rustic charm but now has a far different mission: to provide a "high energy" camp experience in a Christian setting. Youth who attend the 60-acre summer camps will find both swimming and fishing pools, horseback riding, crafts, archery, and drama and art classes, to name just a few. If a staff member comes along with other expertise—like leather crafting or wrestling— Woodbine organizes a class for it, says director Dan Everest, who runs the camp with his wife, Sherry, and up to 50 staff members.

The weeklong summer sessions for youth include morning Bible teaching led by theologically trained staff, with daily praise and worship, much of it done in a contemporary, kid-friendly style. Guests needn't be either Baptist or conservative, but should expect to be introduced "to faith in Christ and how to integrate that faith into their daily lives," Everest says.

Location: A wooded canyon about 7 miles southwest of Sedalia.

Description: An interdenominational, year-round camp run by the Conservative Baptist Association.

Guest Profile: Kids in the summer, Christian groups and churches the rest of the year.

Spiritual Experience: Interactive but with numerous getaway trails.

How to get there: Take I-25 south to the Meadows Parkway exit. Go west past the large outlet center on your right. At the stoplight, take Highway 85 north. Go 5 miles to Sedalia and the intersection with Highway 67. (From some areas of Denver, you may wish to take Santa Fe Drive south, which becomes Highway 85.) Take 67 through town, and drive about 7 miles to the "Woodbine" sign on your left.

He adds that the denomination is in the relaxed middle of the religious spectrum, along the lines of Billy Graham's ministry.

In the fall, winter, and spring, Woodbine welcomes groups of all Christian denominations, from confirmation classes to churches. Accommodations are rustic rather than elegant. Expect to bunk down on army cots in one of seven heated cabins, and be sure to bring your own sleeping bag. The main lodge, which includes a dining room and fireplace, has bunkrooms and the only wintertime restrooms.

The chapel is a large, carpeted A-frame that doubles as a place for recreation and games. Outside of summertime, groups are responsible for their own spiritual programs. The tiered grounds and trails stretch away into the woodlands, making alone-time a distinct possibility, too. But for everyone who comes here, Woodbine will consider that it's done its work if, as Everest puts it, people feel they can be "totally fired up about God and take it back to the city with them."

Sacred Places

33. Red Rocks Park & Amphitheatre

*A*s the first sliver of sun tips the horizon, a gasp rolls over the crowd of 9,000. Then, a chorus of alleluias. Where else—and when else—could such a big congregation come together, worship, and then go their separate ways for the rest of the year? It has to be the fragile hours just before and after dawn on Easter Sunday morning at Red Rocks Amphi-theatre. For more than 50 years, this natural amphitheatre has drawn together people of all and varied faiths to celebrate a common hope in rebirth and the power of resurrection. Every year, the "come one, come all" Easter service manages to surprise everybody with its spiritual impact.

Acoustically perfect for the past 300 million years or so, Red Rocks qualifies as Mother Nature's year-round events center. Its 400-foot-high sandstone slabs, seething ruddy-red with iron, lend a majesty to the place. Evidence suggests that this awesome site has been appreciated for centuries. Artifacts and arrowheads found in the area indicate that Ute Chief Colorow brought his people here to wait out the harsh winter. Like Garden of the Gods (see page 148), the natural walls and insulating properties of the red rocks made this an excellent haven from bitter cold and a serene and protected place to get in touch with other tribes and clans—as well as one's spiritual side.

In 1870, the site got its first official name, Garden of the Angels. That was followed by a sterner moniker, Garden of the Titans. When the city of Denver bought the 640 acres in the late 1920s, the name evolved into the more user-friendly Red Rocks Park. The amphitheatre, based on ancient outdoor theatres of Greece and Sicily, was completed in 1941 and is internationally recognized for its acoustical excellence. After World War II, the Colorado Council of Churches began sponsoring the traditional Easter service, complete with Scripture readings, guest preachers, and full-throated choirs.

To take part in a Red Rocks Easter, set your alarm for several hours before dawn and plan to join the vehicle crawl through the foothills that begins sometime around 5 a.m. Parking for 9,000 may seem daunting, but Red Rocks does it all the time—so it's handled with efficiency and very little fuss.

Of course, you can nurture your spiritual side at Red Rocks individually, all year round. It's open daily, though on an events day it closes to the public at 4 p.m.

The Chapel at Red Rocks, on the south side of the park, is a spectacular site for nondenominational weddings. Red Rocks' staff offers full-service wedding consultations, including everything from budget control to hairstyling. The chapel accommodates 150 visitors and offers a breathtaking view of the Front Range and Denver.

Fifteen miles west of Denver, Red Rocks is well marked from several highway systems. To get there from Denver, go west on I-70 or Highway 6 just beyond town to east C-470. Or take Highway 285 south from Denver, then go west on C-470. Take C-470 to Highway 8 and head west toward the town of Morrison. Follow the signs to the park. For park and events information, go to www.red-rocks.com. For wedding information, call 303-697-0270.

Opposite: The Easter sunrise service at Red Rocks Amphitheatre moves the faithful of all traditions who gather beneath 400-foot-high sandstone rocks.

Region Three:
Mid Front Range

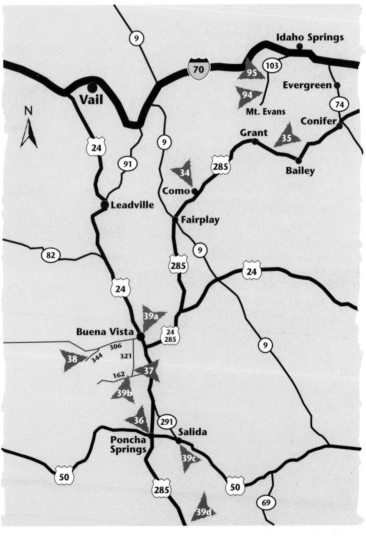

Listing information for 94 above is on p. 239; information for 95 above is on p. 241.

*H*ere are a number of spiritual destinations stretched across a wide and beautiful section of Colorado canvas.

Two retreat centers are tucked along the woodsy canyons that tag alongside Highway 285 as it meanders away from Denver toward the southwest. After you break through Kenosha Pass, the landscape explodes into a saucer-shaped vista ringed with frothy peaks and the Pike National Forest. Soon you'll come upon the 19th-century railroad town of Como and a rustic spiritual getaway whose front yard faces the toothy Tarryall Range.

Continue south into serious Fourteener country. You'll find two more retreat centers hanging around Ivy League neighborhoods in the Collegiate Peaks Range. One, a state-of-the-art camp for youth, is at the foot of Mt. Princeton, and the other, whose specialty is Christian military personnel, is tucked between Mt. Yale and Mt. Princeton.

Retreats

Sacred Places

Retreats

34. Camp Como

Colorado Christian Service Camp
P.O. Box 36
Como, CO 80432
719-836-2382
www.campcomo.com

*T*his camp has the rugged, rangy feel of a Colorado frontier town. Pretty cobblestone paths decorate the long walk in front of the office and main buildings, freshly painted in white and russet red. Set snugly against a forest of trees, the oblong-shaped camp—a mile long but just a quarter mile wide—opens up on one side to a view of the Puma Hills, which stretch into a hazy backdrop of toothy peaks. You'd almost expect "Shane" to come galloping out of the mist.

As a guest, you'll stay in rustic chalets, whose dorm-style accommodations are as rugged as the porch view is dramatic. Inside: Metal bunk beds, some built into the wall. Outside: The plains and mountains shimmer before you. The dining hall doubles as a chapel, though many groups prefer the nearby gym, "which cuts down on the preaching and cooking conflicts," chuckles assistant manager Mark Solomon.

The camp takes its Christian witness seriously. Bible lessons are offered alongside hatchet throwing, which is among a variety of fun activities in the Prospector Tipi, one of the many summer "Kids' Camps." Adults choose from programs such as retreats for men and women or getaways for seniors and families. Modest dress is expected, and campers are to display "Christ-like characteristics in language and conduct."

There's one non-spiritual get-away that guests shouldn't miss while they're here. The old railroad town of Como, just a mile away, is worth more than a browse. It looks like an old prospecting town, with hardy old buildings clustered on the plains. Many have been lovingly restored, like the Como Gen'l Store and Como Mercantile, where you can find everything from groceries and video rentals to antiques and fishing gear.

Many tourists stop just to tour the town's massive 19th-century stone roundhouse, the switching place for the narrow-gauge railroad that once chugged through here.

Location: 75 miles southwest of Denver, 85 miles northwest of Colorado Springs, with a panoramic view of the Puma Hills and Tarryall Range.

Description: A rustic, all-purpose, activities-oriented Christian camp.

Guest Profile: Youth, adults, and groups, with special retreats available for women, men, seniors, families, etc.

Spiritual Experience: Geared to groups, but grounds and nearby town of Como offer interesting spots to explore.

How to get there: Get on Highway 285. (In Denver it masquerades as Hampden Avenue.) The camp is between two tiny gulps of a town on 285: 10 miles north of Fairplay and 6.5 miles south of Jefferson. Look carefully for the sign pointing west to Como/Boreas Pass. You can see the town of Como from the highway. Follow the road into town. Stay on the blacktop and watch for small oblong "Camp Como" signs. The road turns to dirt, and you have 1 mile farther to go.

Built in 1881, the roundhouse was the center of activity of this railroad mecca, which peaked in 1910, the year a cave-in closed the Alpine Tunnel. In 1983 the roundhouse was declared a national historic site, and it still sits, a historic treasure, on these rugged plains.

35. Camp Santa Maria

P.O. Box 19020
Denver, CO 80219
Seasonal camp address:
Drawer D
Shawnee, CO 80475
303-742-0823

Guests dip off a busy highway into a lovely forested retreat site that used to be the 19th-century resort hotel called Cassells. Some of the buildings still recall early days on this site, such as the hushed frame chapel, suffused with the fragrance of old wood and graced with a traditional altar. It's a meditative getaway from another era to sit on the chapel's old wood benches as dappled daylight struggles through the old miter-shaped windows. Before you in the dusty gloom are early 20th-century statues of a blue-robed Mary, a welcoming Jesus, and Joseph, whispering to the Christ Child.

Another Camp Santa Maria statue has become a prominent landmark in the area. High above the camp is a statue of Jesus, arms outstretched, which to many recalls the famous and similar statue in Rio de Janeiro. This one is visible from miles away if you know where to look. From the camp it's accessible by a very brisk getaway hike up a rugged mountainside, which rises hundreds of feet from the gorge. Behind you, unseen but not far away, is 12,871-foot Mt. Logan.

Location: In Grant, about 50 miles southwest of Denver.

Description: A nondenominational retreat center run by Catholic Charities of the Archdiocese of Denver.

Guest Profile: Youth during summer, including inner-city kids, and adult groups other seasons. Not open for individual retreats.

Spiritual Experience: Surroundings make for solitude possibilities, which include a towering mountainside and a lake. Traffic sounds from Highway 285 are inevitable.

How to get there: Get on Highway 285 (In Denver it masquerades as Hampden Avenue.) Set your odometer at zero at Bailey; you are 9 miles from the camp. Watch for the eye-blink of a town called Shawnee, 5.2 miles from camp. The statue of Jesus becomes visible momentarily above, to your right, about 3 miles past Shawnee. Slow down; the entrance comes up fast on your right. If you miss it, there's another one a few dozen feet ahead. If you're coming from the north on 285, you're 10 miles from camp when you break Kenosha Pass. At the town of Grant, you have 1.6 miles to go. The camp is on your left. (At Grant you have a rugged option available for vaulting over the mountains to I-70 and Georgetown: Follow the sign to Guanella Pass/ Georgetown, and you'll be rewarded with 24 scenic miles over rough dirt road with high cliff exposures.)

Catholic Charities manages the camp, although the summer youth program, running June through August, is rigorously nondenominational and designed to appeal to children of all faiths. Adult groups (which bring their own programs and leadership) get their chance from mid-March through May and in September and October. The camp is closed from November through the beginning of March. Adult groups may find room in the summer, but that's based on availability.

Once here, guests bunk down—literally—in heated cabins that sleep 28. A bathhouse is in the middle of camp. The rustic dining hall is peppered with holy pictures and has a view up the mountainside. As more funds become available, the camp is upgrading its tennis courts and general activities area. But among the things funding can't buy are the chances to visit a lovely lake tucked into one corner of the site, and to hear the sounds of the "North Fork of the South Platte" as it tumbles and grumbles its way through the sun- and shadow-streaked campgrounds.

36. The Christian Adventure Company

P.O. Box 187
Poncha Springs, CO 81242
719-530-0174
E-mail: tcac@chaffee.net
www.thechristianadventure.com

*T*his Christian camping ministry, which operates in the summer months, takes adults and youth on backcountry adventures such as backpacking, camping, mountain biking, and caving. With every sundown comes a faith-based roundup of the day's activities and the ways they shed insight on one's Christian witness. The best example is rappelling: the mountaineering trick of "walking" down a sheer drop while held by a rope. As you survey 300 feet of air beneath your feet, do you trust your rope? Likewise, as you survey the scary breadth of your life's problems, do you trust your God? Those are the kinds of questions that Rev. James ("Gibby") Gilbert and his staff will pose to you campside, at the end of a long and stimulating backcountry day.

Location: Somewhere in the wilderness of Chaffee County.

Description: A weeklong, Christian-themed backcountry experience. The highlight of each week is summiting a mountain (no technical climbing experience required).

Guest Profile: For well-conditioned people who want to add a Christian dimension to their adventure.

Spiritual Experience: Expect to stretch body and soul.

How to get there: When you sign up, you'll get directions to that week's wilderness area. Most groups meet in Salida, which is about 5 miles from the main office in Poncha Springs.

The program is group-oriented, and 20 is considered the ideal number. Individuals and smaller groups are welcome to apply but should expect to be folded into a larger group. This popular summer program is usually booked solid by January, so it's best to get hold of Gilbert by late fall of the previous year. (He sets Christmas as his deadline to get out reservation forms.)

The ministry uses state-licensed outfitters and works under the guidelines of the U.S. Forest Service. Guests receive a handbook on what to bring, which is limited to personal items. That includes a Bible. The program supplies all the major gear, including tents, sleeping bags, and backpacks. The week is built around summiting a peak, which is usually in the 12,000-foot range. No technical climbing is required, but prepare to negotiate high boulder fields and do some serious scrambling to the top.

Each day is built around spiritual themes, and the evening discussions include such relevant ideas as hearing each other's burdens. (There's a day of rest, too.) Several hours are devoted to daily Bible reading and prayer time. Leave all electronic gear at home, says Gilbert, and instead tune in "to the birds, brooks, and wind." On the final day, your hardy backcountry week is rewarded with a farewell restaurant dinner in Salida.

37. Frontier Ranch

22150 County Road #322
P.O. Box 2025
Buena Vista, CO 81211
719-395-4111
Fax: 719-395-4115

*C*onsider this the Disneyland of Christian youth camps and retreat centers. Staff here cheerfully accept the comparison. Since the founding of Young Life, the parent organization, in 1941, the goal has been to spare nothing to bring Jesus Christ to generations endangered by the worldly pleasures of the modern age. Here, young people absorb the Christian experience while enjoying, in a wholesome setting, the best the culture—and Colorado—has to offer.

This resort-quality complex boasts a gift shop, state-of-the-art amphitheatre, year-round pool, and a dining room that looks like it could fit as the Hall of the Mountain King. Its multitiered, well-groomed grounds hang on a cliff side overlooking Chalk Creek and deep mountain gorges. Looming just beyond is the Sangre de Cristo Range and Mt. Princeton, one of the most graceful in a veritable ballet corps of nearby Fourteeners.

In the midst of this mountain aerie is the most revered building of all—the sturdy, modest, and still much-used log cabin home where the Young Life dream began. Here, in a living room overlooking a vista (besides 14,197-foot Mt. Princeton, Tabeguache, Mt. Shavano, and Mt. Antero ring the immediate neighborhood), founder Jim Rayburn and a group of fellow evangelical Christian leaders knelt on the cherry-colored southwestern carpet and prayed all night for direction. They wanted God to tell them how to begin a movement to bring Jesus Christ to young people coming of age in the moral upheavals that followed World War II. The answer they got was beyond their wildest dreams. Young Life now reaches hundreds of thousands of youth worldwide.

While Young Life camps abound, Frontier Ranch has remained the archetypal example of how to use worldly blessings to spread the Christian message. The goal "is to enable kids to come out of their environment and give them the opportunity to have the best week of their lives," says Joe MacInnis, guest services coordinator. "We don't want only church kids, we want all types of kids." The high-activity camp offers rugged sports such as mountain climbing and rappelling, and a posh game room for indoor sports such as pool and Ping-Pong. There's a state-of-the-art sound system for get-togethers and skits. While there's no chapel per se, the atmosphere draws kids in to be "open to hear the Gospel," says MacInnis. "Everything we do surrounds that."

Location: About 10 miles from Buena Vista.

Description: A bustling, resort-quality camp that combines Christian witness with activities and lots of interaction.

Guest Profile: Youth in summer; churches, families, and groups the rest of the year.

Spiritual Experience: The terrain (and staff) encourages solitary getaways in this majestic setting of Fourteeners in the Collegiate Range.

How to get there: Get to Buena Vista. (General access is off Highway 285, but you'll have to exit onto Highway 24 to get into town.) In the center of town look for the one stoplight intersection, which is at Main Street. Go west on Main. Drive about a mile and look for County Road 321, which veers off to the left. (It may also be marked as Rodeo Road.) Follow that 8 miles, then take 322 right.

38. Spring Canyon Christian Camp and Conference Center

P.O. Box 2047
Buena Vista, CO 81211
1-888-663-1417
Fax: 719-395-6364
www.ocfusa.org

People who come here for weddings, family reunions, seminars, or a quiet, prayer-filled getaway will surely leave with unforgettable memories of this lovely, Christian-centered retreat haven at the base of 14,197-foot Mt. Princeton.

But first dibs go to the military. This is a family retreat center of the Officers' Christian Fellowship, which purchased the property in 1962. The fellowship includes men and women from all branches of the armed forces who are committed to living, and evangelizing, their Christian belief in Jesus Christ within the military lifestyle.

The quaint central lodge and office is dedicated to Captain Hartley Holmes, a British officer who, at the height of World War II, launched the first gathering of Christians serving in the British armed forces. He encouraged the founding of an American branch and is memorialized by name, plaque, and a stalwart, stiff-upper-lipped portrait in the worship area of the lodge. The rest of the grounds, tucked in the shadow of the towering Collegiate Peaks, are also imbued with classic rustic charm and resort-quality accommodations. Pathways meander over babbling mountain brooks. Spring water, which gushes out between 400 and 800 gallons a minute, is bottled and sold as some of the purest in the state.

The cabins are hefty, classic log cabins that look like they could withstand battalions. They've been redone in charming style, with touches that include stone fireplaces, carpeting, and skylights. One cabin, outfitted with a sleigh bed and pretty curtains, is specially outfitted for the handicapped. There's even a "honeymoon cabin" set in a more secluded area beside the camp's ever-present mountain spring. Guests can plunge into no end of physical activities, including kayaking, trout fishing, and hiking. Some set their sights on vanquishing The Hook, a 13,000-foot granite oddity that pierces the nearby sky. But the main goal here is to provide a place to quietly seek God.

In 2000, the Spring Canyon's directors presented a plan to expand the uses of the camp for more evangelical outreach. It calls for reaching out aggressively to military families to present "God's blueprint for living" in all seasons of life—including to military youth, who face mounting secular pressures in the 21st century.

Location: About 8 miles from Buena Vista.

Description: A year-round Christian retreat complex "where your spiritual strength can be renewed and where you can celebrate the goodness of our Savior, Jesus Christ."

Guest Profile: First to the U.S. military, through the Officers' Christian Fellowship, then to groups, families, and individuals.

Spiritual Experience: Solitude is encouraged in a setting that also offers conference space and an array of outdoor activities.

How to get there: The main north/south route through Buena Vista is US Highway 24. The town's stoplight intersection is Main Street, or County Road 306, which becomes Forest Road 306. Take that west about 7 miles. Look for signs for Spring Canyon and Cottonwood Lake. Turn left onto Forest Road 344, go about a mile, and look for the sign on the right.

Sacred Places

39. Hot Springs & Sacred Things

Photo courtesy of Neil Seitz

*H*ot springs speak for themselves. Come upon these serene natural wonders, and chances are you'll need no sermon to tell you that these are

Valley View Hot Springs in Villa Grove, near the north end of the Rio Grande National Forest.

places of healing, havens for meditation, and deeply sacred destinations to ancient peoples. "In the Native American belief system, hot springs held a special meaning beyond the curative powers of hot water," says Deborah Frazier George, author of *Colorado's Hot Springs*. "To many tribes, the hot springs were a contact point for mother earth, a place where divine powers reached out, embraced them warmly and gave them a physical reassurance of their link to something greater."

Colorado is a treasure trove of hot springs. In this area of the Mid Front Range and northern San Luis Valley there are five major ones, each with its own haunting history. Ute tribes revered these places and were regular visitors, until driven away from their sanctuaries by 19th-century settlers. Well before the turn of the last century, the tribes had been definitively goaded onto government reservations. Surely those who escape today to these ancient places of meditation and healing will feel a jolt of sorrow for the Utes' loss.

North to south, here they are. All details hail from George's book:

39a. Cottonwood Hot Springs

Buena Vista. Legend has it that the Utes put a curse upon all future owners who would try to revive this hot springs, according to Cathy Manning, who bought the run-down property in 1986. (A 19th-century homeopathic center and an early-20th-century spa both burned to the ground.) So far, Manning has dodged the curse, although it's been a long haul to make these springs what she envisioned—a place of rejuvenation and retreat from an intense world. For more information, call 719-395-6434.

Cottonwood Hot Springs, near Buena Vista, a historic gathering place of the Utes and today open year-round for rejuvenation of body and spirit.

39b. Mount Princeton Hot Springs Resort

Nathrop. The Utes still held title to the land, writes George, when a surveyor put dibs on these springs in the mid-1800s. Believe it or not, the bathhouse used today was built in 1850. For more information, call 719-395-2361.

39c. Salida Hot Springs Aquatic Center

Salida. Poncha Springs is the genesis for 45 hot springs, which today are channeled into the public pool in Salida, 5 miles away on US 50. It's the largest indoor hot springs pool in Colorado, according to George. For more information, call 719-539-6738.

39d. Valley View Hot Springs

Villa Grove. A trove of arrowheads and artifacts proves the Utes were here—a lot. In the '60s, hippies took over. Today, the hot springs is members-only on weekends. The waiting list is long and the setting primeval, says George, marked by the sounds of wind, trees, and birds. For more information, call 719-256-4315.

39e. Mineral Hot Springs Spa

Moffat. This was a very popular hot springs to Ute tribes, judging by uncovered artifacts. It's equally popular to retreatants visiting Crestone (see Region 5, "Crestone and the San Luis Valley"). For more information, call 719-256-4328 (see map on p. 156).

Other Spiritual Destinations

Camp Id-Ra-Ha-Je

P.O. Box 360, Bailey, CO 80421-0360; 303-838-5668 or 1-877-838-5668 (www.idrahaje.org): A year-round Christian adventure camp with 253 acres of land and a complex that includes dorm-style and family cabins. Programs for teens, families, and adults. "Our goal is to provide an environment where each camper will grow physically, spiritually, emotionally, and mentally," says the colorful brochure. There's a sister camp on the Western Slope (see Camp Id-Ra-Ha-Je West, page 202). Both have crafted a name that describes their mission: I'D RA-ther HA-ve JE-sus. Staff is screened carefully and prayerfully, say longtime directors John F. and Lindy Obrecht.

Frontier Ranch near Buena Vista, where the Young Life evangelical Christian camps were founded.

Region Four:
Southern Front Range

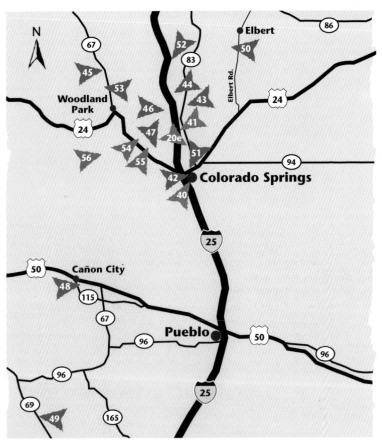

Listing information for 20e above is on p. 67.

ooking for a backcountry spiritual experience but don't want to drive backcountry miles? This is just the region for planning a secluded spiritual getaway not too far from city bustle.

Thanks to its tumultuous geography, the Southern Front Range is a wonderland carved and crisscrossed with canyons, forests, and mountain trails, punctuated by urban areas. Retreats and sanctuaries are found almost anywhere, from shrouded forests to busy residential streets.

You may feel as far away as the Yukon just by traveling northwest of Colorado Springs about 25 miles, where Woodland Park and Divide mark a cluster of religious retreats tucked miles away on dirt roads. Meanwhile, you can get much the same sense of seclusion and solitude at centers located deep in the woodland, but only a few miles off Interstate 25. More spiritual destinations mark the way southward toward Pueblo and Cañon City. And the metro area of Colorado Springs offers a gamut of sanctuaries, retreats, and sacred places. Some have an international heft: One is the center for a worldwide prayer movement, and another is the center for research into one of the world's most enduring—and controversial—religious mysteries of all time. Some offer help using modern psycho-spiritual tools; others simply give you trails to wander and the encouragement to pray.

Sanctuaries

40. Turin Shroud Center of Colorado

P.O. Box 25326
Colorado Springs, CO 80918
719-599-5755
www.shroudofturin.com

*I*s it a museum? A walk through time? A religious experience? Any, or all three. In an office suite located in a business park, John and Rebecca Jackson open the doors to a fascinating mystery: Does the Shroud of Turin contain the imprint of the face and body of Jesus? No doubt you've heard about the controversy, pro and con. Ever since the eerie image was discovered in France on a photographic negative in 1898, science has debated what it means. No sooner has one side claimed that carbon dating proves the shroud a 14th-century hoax than supporters refute the claim with burn analysis and isotopic enrichment data. Guests here have the chance to make up their own minds by grilling two of the world's leading researchers on the shroud. Skeptics are as welcome as the devout.

The center is the life work of a retired Navy physicist, Dr. John P. Jackson, a Denver native who has been one of the original researchers and supporters of the shroud's authenticity since the 1970s. Rebecca S. Jackson, his wife, is an expert on first-century Hebraic laws and customs. Both lecture extensively around the world and have met with Pope John Paul II, a shroud supporter. While the Jacksons hypothesize that the shroud is genuine, they say they are dedicated to proving it with absolute scientific rigor—and that means years of meticulous research. Based on their collaboration with scientists and researchers around the world, the Jacksons have reconstructed the exhaustive process for guests.

In a warren of rooms, guests gaze on a full-sized exact reproduction of the shroud, photographed with such high-powered lenses that they can see it down to its linen fibers—just like they could on the original, if it weren't under guard and locked away in Italy. Guests peer into glass counters containing pertinent crucifixion data, such as replicas of first-century Roman nails and crowns of thorns. They wander past startling re-creations,

Location: Colorado Springs.

Description: A sanctuary dedicated to research on the shroud as the burial cloth of Jesus Christ; run by Dr. John P. Jackson and Rebecca S. Jackson, experts in shroud research. The Jacksons also lead tours and retreats to Turin, Italy, when the shroud is on public display.

Guest Profile: Anyone with an interest in the Shroud of Turin—or in unsolved mysteries.

Spiritual Experience: Profound, for those who believe the shroud is genuine. For others, a provocative journey through Judaic-Christian religious history or an up-close look at a highly publicized scientific controversy.

How to get there: Tours by appointment only. Get directions when you make an appointment.

too, such as full-sized models hanging from a cross (to depict body weight and other physical data). The models were based on volunteers at the Air Force Academy, where Jackson once taught physics.

The 90-minute, step-by-step guided tour includes Rebecca Jackson's data on first-century dining and burial practices, which the Jacksons say is crucial to understanding some of the inexplicable findings, ranging from the way the cloth was folded to infinitesimal stains on the linen. Whether or not you come away a believer, the tour offers a front-row look into one of the most provocative religious mysteries of all time.

41. World Prayer Center

11005 State Highway 83 (attn: Rev. Peter Sekovski)
Colorado Springs, CO 80921
719-536-9100
Fax: 719-548-9000

*E*ver wish there was a place to go to in the middle of the night to pray? Thanks to the combined vision of two evangelical Christian leaders, there is such a place—a veritable monument to prayer, sprawling over acres of land just off the Interstate. This huge complex, which resembles a sleek, modern office park, is the vision of Ted Haggard, pastor of the adjacent New Life Church, and C. Peter Wagner, founder of Global Harvest Ministries, whose mission is worldwide evangelization.

Any time of the day or night visitors may enter this 500-seat, auditorium-style "chapel" whose bank of windows opens onto the grandeur of Pikes Peak and the Front Range. But the men's vision is even bigger: They want to link the prayers of each visitor here to 50 million people in 120 countries. The upshot is not just a place to pray, but an international network of information and links to prayer needs around the world.

Location: The north end of Colorado Springs, on the east side of I-25.

Description: An all-night prayer chapel with overnight accommodations and an adjacent church.

Guest Profile: All welcome.

Spiritual Experience: A place to pause and pray.

How to get there: The complex is just off the Interquest exit (Highway 83, Academy Boulevard) in Colorado Springs.

And that's not all.

In the evangelical Christian tradition of praying with insistent, round-the-clock intensity, the complex offers private overnight accommodations. These range from small, monklike "prayer closets" furnished with little more than a bed and dresser, to hotel-quality "prayer rooms," to suites that resemble the plush business accommodations at a high-end hotel. These are often booked for church groups and large prayer teams. (Costs range from a few dollars for a prayer closet up to the price of a budget motel.)

For those with less time but no less intensity, the auditorium/chapel may provide inspiration of its own. A huge globe of planet Earth, 15 feet in diameter, slowly rotates one revolution an hour, underscoring the center's international mission. Music is piped in from the cutting-edge sound system in back. (Visitors are welcome to fiddle with the volume control.) Wired with the latest technology, the auditorium is also used for huge teleconferences and leadership training for the 7,000-member New Life Church, which is on adjacent property.

The grounds are landscaped to be prayer-friendly. Visitors may flock to a number of quiet sitting areas overlooking the Front Range and Pikes Peak, surrounded by gardens stocked with exotic plants. The complex itself is flanked by the flags of 54 nations, yet another reminder that here, when it comes to prayer, no man is an island.

Retreats

42. Benet Hill Monastery

2555 North Chelton Road
Colorado Springs, CO 80921
719-633-0655

*A*t first, your destination looks very much like a high school out of the '60s—which it is. This former girls' school is now home to a charter school and the headquarters and offices of the monastery. Behind the building is a lovely expanse of groomed grounds where guests spend most of their time. The grounds include handsome buildings for the novices (sisters in training) as well as nursing home facilities for nuns at the sunset of their lives. Guests stay in "St. Luke's" building, in comfortable single bedrooms with baths down the hall. There's room for about seven guests at a time. Guests may also stay at "St. Benedict's," a ranch home across the street.

In the main building, you'll enter a classic high school foyer with speckled marble floors and a double-stair balustrade that carried several generations of class-bound students to and fro. At the foot of the staircase, a lovely centerpiece of greenery and a trickling waterfall provide a meditative hush. The main building has two dining rooms and is also the place where guests will come for spiritual direction and take part in classes, which include an array of programs on topics such as scripture, mysticism, and centering prayer.

Here, guests may pursue classes, taught by various spiritual leaders and scholars, that range from Reiki energy work to examinations of truths of Christianity or Buddhism, to retreats that cater to couples, caregivers, and even lovers of fishing and hiking. On the grounds, guests may join the nuns in their carpeted chapel as they say their daily "Divine Office," the centuries-old prayers of the Catholic Church. The chapel, a melding of modern and classic, is decorated with stained glass and paintings. A bank of wide windows opens to green bluffs. The chapel's modular style allows the nuns to rearrange the furniture to accommodate talks and lectures. The Blessed Sacrament in the tabernacle is placed behind a screen to the side. The nuns dress in modern street garb and offer their own contemporary, nondenominational spiritual programs ranging from workshops on prayer to dreamwork.

This is a residential setting, so if you long for the rustic charms of the backcountry, the nuns suggest driving about 15 miles to the Benet Pines Retreat Center, which is also run by their order (see page 122).

Location: Colorado Springs.

Description: A residential retreat center.

Guest Profile: All welcome.

Spiritual Experience: The campus provides getaway space, but be aware that the center is located on a residential street.

How to get there: Take I-25 to the Fillmore exit at Colorado Springs. Go east. Cross Union. Fillmore changes to North Circle Drive. At the stoplight, which is at Holiday (about a mile from the change to North Circle), go left (north). Go a few blocks to the end of the street. That's Chelton. Go right (east) about three blocks to the monastery, which is a big old former high school on your left.

43. Benet Pines Retreat Center

15780 Highway 83
Colorado Springs, CO 80921
719-495-2574
Fax: 719-471-0403
www.geocities.com/wellesley/2815

The towering pines of Colorado's Black Forest beckon guests into this low-key spiritual getaway. As you turn up the dirt road off the highway, you enter a well-groomed forest that hides myriad retreat secrets, including tiny hermitages, Zen gardens, and a stone-marked labyrinth. At the end of the road is a simple ranch house, which serves as office and home for the contemporary Benedictine nuns who run the center. Dressed, like their guests, in backcountry garb of sweaters and slacks, the nuns offer spiritual direction and organize talks and seminars on subjects ranging from prayer to dream interpretation.

The nuns say they have worked hard to present an innovative spiritual fare, harvested from ancient Christian traditions, modern-day spirituality, and psychotherapy techniques. One nun offers massage therapy and Reiki energy sessions. Classic spiritual direction is based on their faith and their "relationship with the Lord," according to a retreat brochure. Spiritual directors are trained in Vatican II theology, dreamwork, and accessing the active imagination.

Location: A half-hour drive north of downtown Colorado Springs.

Description: A retreat center run by Benedictine nuns for people "to discover more fully God and themselves."

Guest Profile: All welcome, individually or in church or nonprofit groups.

Spiritual Experience: Solitude is a cornerstone of this forest experience, whether you come here to be alone or to take part in a "directed retreat" organized by one of the nuns or a retreat leader.

How to get there: From I-25, north of Colorado Springs, take the Interquest exit (Highway 83, Academy Boulevard). Drive north 6 or 7 miles. Slow down when you see a small sign for Stage Coach Road—the Benet Pines entrance sign comes up fast on your left.

Guests may also choose their own paths—literally. The woods stretch out, waiting to be plumbed in silence. Walk the wood-chipped paths deeper into a sentinel of pines. Free of any obscuring underbrush, the clean-limbed pines rise and fall over hill and dale and give the illusion of going on forever.

Eventually the walker comes upon two distinctive features: a Zen garden and a labyrinth. Zen gardens are minimalist oases designed for meditation and marked by simple benches and arched bridges. The labyrinth is an eye-catching maze-like puzzle, about ankle level, built on the pattern of the 800-year-old labyrinth set in the floor of the cathedral in Chartres, France. The walker begins at the entrance and winds back and forth until reaching the center. Devotees say the ancient exercise promotes a meditative technique that helps untangle life's problems.

Day guests are welcome. As night falls, overnighters head for the simple, ranch-style cabins, which offer several cozy rustic bedrooms (two to a bedroom) flanking a kitchen and living room with stone fireplace. Most overnighters, who may number as many as 18, stay in the cabins. For the single-minded, there are four one-person hermitages scattered throughout the woods, simply furnished with a cot-bed and dresser.

The chapel area is more of a small meditation room. Guests may join the sisters for Catholic Mass at the local church, Our Lady of the Pines. There are also opportunities to live in one of the hermitages for a sabbatical period. "This offers the individual time for long periods of reflective leisure to pray, read, commune with Mother Earth, and to enter into the monastic rhythm of the Benedictine community," the brochure explains.

44. Black Forest Camp and Conference Center

780 East Baptist Road
Colorado Springs, CO 80921
719-488-3750
www.bfccc.org

*I*n 1946 a group of Baptists began scouting for the ideal site to put a church campground in Colorado. Their attention was drawn to a fox farm north of Colorado Springs. In 1950 a picnic lunch launched this popular center, which now balances recreational activities with opportunities for spiritual getaways all along its hilly and forested paths.

Many of the original cabins, now bordering on 100 years of age, are still used for summer youth housing. The other overnight accommodations range from tents to hotel-style rooms in the main lodge. Buildings clustered around the camp offer everything in between. As just two examples in an array of combinations, there are private rooms with full baths, and also what's called "intimate lodging" for smaller families, with one double bed and a single bunk. There is no main chapel, but a short hike from the cluster of main buildings takes you to three outdoor spiritual sites, located on land that has been kept in its natural, rough-and-ready state.

One site is unique indeed: In a very pretty modern gazebo, staff have placed what they called the "A-Tree," signifying Alpha, which recalls Jesus

Location: In rolling hills and forest about 20 miles north of downtown Colorado Springs, with a clear view of Pikes Peak and the Air Force Academy.

Description: "A Christ-centered, spirit-filled facility for all ages and churches" run by the American Baptist Church of the Rocky Mountains.

Guest Profile: Youth and family reunions in the summer, church and small groups, couples, and individuals in the winter.

Spiritual Experience: Solitude getaways along the winding trails and at three outdoor chapels.

How to get there: From I-25, take Baptist Road (Exit 158) east. Drive 1.8 miles to Kingswood Road, which only goes left. There will be a camp sign there too. You'll see a large housing development directly opposite the roadway. Drive another 0.7 mile to the camp entrance, and another half mile up a dirt road to the lodge.

Christ's words in the Bible: "I am the Alpha and the Omega" (that is, the beginning and end). This natural wonder, a large tree trunk curled in the shape of an "A" about 5 feet high, was found on the grounds decades ago and has been lovingly restored and oiled. There are two other outdoor sites with benches, called High Vespers and Low Vespers, where guests can come to pray.

Although this friendly camp is set up for groups and conference-goers, assistant director Melissa Morton says individuals and couples are also welcome. (If that's your profile, you may want to ask for the Ripley Cabin, the main residence of the former fox farm.) Everything, of course, depends on availability. Morton says some individuals—"regulars" who return every year—have made this their place to meet up with friends and family, thereby combining the joys of reunion with the spiritual peace of a retreat.

45. Camp Elim

5567 County Road 78
Woodland Park, CO 80863
719-687-2030
www.campelim.com

*Y*ou'd be hard-pressed to find a cleaner, better-groomed complex. Rising straight and tall from the scrubbed groundcover, ponderosa pines and Douglas firs stand sentinel in this forest primeval. Under the forested shadows, a cluster of sturdy, rustic cabins forms a cozy scene. The neat and compact atmosphere is probably the direct result of its easy care, thanks to Elim's relatively small size—just 18 acres, says director Jay Brady.

However, there's national forest land rising on three sides, making any number of outdoor activities available. But the essence of the camp is the spiritual experience it offers groups. At the heart of that experience is a brand-new and very striking chapel, a majestic, rustic building that looks something like a log cabin cathedral.

Inside, the scene is spiritually low key. There's a beautiful stone fireplace but no cross—the symbol is not customary among Plymouth Brethren. The camp limits its groups, which can adhere to a mission statement proclaiming the Bible as "the inerrant word of God and Jesus as Savior and Lord." Accommodations are very rustic and dormitory/bunk style throughout. The dining room seats about 80 under its wagon-wheel chandeliers.

Location: About 25 miles from Colorado Springs in the Pike National Forest.

Description: A camp offering spiritual getaways to church groups.

Guest Profile: Church groups of 30 or more. During the summer, Elim runs its own programs. The camp is associated with the Plymouth Brethren but all denominations are welcome.

Spiritual Experience: Geared to providing a "retreat environment."

How to get there: From I-25 in Colorado Springs, take the Highway 24 exit west (Cimarron, Exit 141, with additional signs for Manitou Springs and Pikes Peak). Drive 19 miles to the center of the town of Woodland Park. Pass several stoplights, and turn right (north) onto Highway 67. Drive 7 miles. Look for Painted Rocks Campground on the left. Take that road a half mile to the campground entrance.

46. The Franciscan Retreat Center at Mount St. Francis

7740 Deer Hill Grove
Colorado Springs, CO 80919
719-598-5486
Fax: 719-260-8044
www.franciscanretreatcenter.org

$\mathcal{S}$t. Francis of Assisi, patron saint of animals, must take a personal interest in his namesake retreat center. That's because the first thing you may notice as you enter these groomed grounds is the welcoming committee: herds of gentle-eyed deer clustered around the winding drive as if they were just waiting to say hello. Mysteriously enough, on the first day of deer-hunting season these lovely creatures begin to multiply on the grounds, says retreat director Sister Christine Hayes. At first, that may seem as unexplainable as the annual return of the swallows to Capistrano. Then again, you may understand why the deer consider this a safe haven after you've spent some time here yourself.

The secret may be that this center combines simplicity and comfort with what's known as Franciscan hospitality. (The history of the grounds may inspire you, too.) This is the site of a 19th-century tuberculosis sanatorium developed by Woodmen Insurance Co., a firm now memorialized in place and street names. Ask to see the old photographs lining one of the meeting rooms. As you'll see, the grounds were once covered by hundreds of tiny wooden "tepees," each a home to a TB sufferer.

Today, you get your own room, too—but in far better style, complete with private bath (most retreat centers have communal bathrooms). Rooms for the disabled are also available. While the style is simple—bed, chair, dresser—your room, like the entire complex, has been charmingly outfitted with exquisite, early-20th-century furniture rescued from the old convent days. Buffed and shining, the sturdy chairs and dressers lend a gracious note to this well-renovated center.

Groups will appreciate the spacious reception areas, meeting rooms, and a great dining hall. Everything has that crisp, updated feel of well-maintained property. Since acquiring the land in 1954, the sisters have prudently sold off a great deal of the surrounding acreage they didn't need, and then used the money to keep their own campus well-heeled, indeed. There is, for example, a new sisters' chapel, where

Location: Colorado Springs, adjacent to the Air Force Academy.

Description: A place of rest, reflection, and prayer located on grounds that embrace local history, lands for wandering, and the regional headquarters of the Sisters of St. Francis.

Guest Profile: Groups, churches, and individuals; any and all denominations welcome. Weekends are usually taken up with groups and organizations; individuals have better luck during the week.

Spiritual Experience: Excellent opportunities for solitude (silence is usually maintained unless there is a large group) plus many walking get-aways on the grounds.

How to get there: Take I-25 to Woodmen Road. From the exit, go west half a mile to the stoplight. Take that first right, which keeps you on Woodmen. Go 3.1 miles straight to Mount St. Francis.

you are welcome for daily Mass in the morning and prayer throughout the day. Those seeking solitude will appreciate the chapel's hushed atmosphere and its updated-yet-traditional feel, with cushioned chairs and pullout kneelers. The boldly colored stained glass depicts scenes in the life of St. Francis. The Blessed Sacrament is centered behind the altar in a modern "sunburst" tabernacle that recalls St. Francis's canticle to the sun.

The outdoor grounds, with blacktop pathways curling throughout the campus, are perfect for wandering. For the truly solitude-minded, there's adjacent meadowland. On football weekends you can share in the convivial spirit of the nearby Air Force Academy, which sends squadrons of jets overhead at the start of each home game.

Whether you're here for seminars or your own private retreat, there's enough space to make your getaway exactly as you want it. (Groups have the main dining room; individuals eat with the sisters in their dining room.) The hilly, multitiered campus begs to be explored: The buildings, once home to the sanatorium's staff, have been lovingly restored. The sisters even rescued one of the old TB tepees, which a neighbor was using as a utility shed. Freshly painted and restored to museum-quality condition, the tepee lures you to peer inside to see how a tuberculosis victim once lived, year-round: sleeping on an iron bed, within arm's reach of a simple washstand and dresser. The sobering sight may help with one's meditation on suffering, as well as with gratitude for one's blessings. Compared to those long-gone residents, you will certainly have a better time here.

47. Glen Eyrie Conference Center

P.O. Box 6000
Colorado Springs, CO 80934
719-598-1212
Fax: 719-272-7432

*Y*ou came to Glen Eyrie seeking a spiritual getaway, but you may wonder if you stumbled onto a 16th-century Brigadoon. Is that a Tudor king you see, galloping from his castle grounds, over rustic bridges and

Description: A history-laden, high-quality resort complex with religious underpinnings.

Guest Profile: All welcome; a major specialty is religious organizations and large pastors' retreats.

Spiritual Experience: The grounds invite solitude and meditation.

How to get there: From I-25, take the Garden of the Gods exit west to 30th Street. Turn left. Go less than a quarter mile and look for the sign on the right. You'll know you're heading in the right location, as a craggy orange peak looms before you.

past his herd of bighorn sheep? Only the king requires your imagination. The castle, the bridges, and the hauntingly lovely groomed grounds are real—and for that matter, so are the sheep. Nestled, appropriately enough, against Garden of the Gods Park, Glen Eyrie is a one-of-a-kind experience now open for individual stays, group retreats, and conferences. But it began as a love gift to a bride.

This is the 19th-century estate of railroad magnate and Civil War hero General William Jackson Palmer. When his beloved wife died in 1894, he dedicated himself to finishing the property in regal style as a tribute to her memory. But only Palmer himself could keep the full majesty of his idea intact. After his death in 1909 the estate was sold, resold, and chopped up and considered as a possible country club, cattle ranch, or summer home.

Nothing quite clicked until a Christian organization, the Navigators, bought Palmer's love gift in 1953 at the urging of the Rev. Billy Graham. The famed preacher had considered the estate for his international headquarters. The Navigators, begun in 1933, are dedicated to following Jesus Christ as Lord and Savior. The name is based on Paul's letter to Timothy, in which he exhorts those who hear the truth to find reliable witnesses (that is, navigators) to steer others toward the truth of the Gospel.

Today, Glen Eyrie exudes a Christian message in an unobtrusive, genteel way. More obvious is the posh "clubbiness." Walk into the castle anteroom—where a knight in full armor greets you. Fellow guests burrow in elegant, overstuffed chairs, reading newspapers as in a fine English country estate. You may stay in the castle or in one of the many resort-quality lodges on the estate. Meditate while strolling down paths that wind through pine-studded grounds and the rosy-orange, razor-backed cliffs made famous at Garden of the Gods.

In keeping with Palmer's romantic tradition, the center offers an array of charming rituals, including English teas, six-course dinners, and Christmas madrigals. Tours are available for a small fee. There is a gift store as well as a bookstore featuring Bibles and gift items.

48. Holy Cross Abbey

P.O. Box 1510
Cañon City, CO 81215-1510
719-275-8631

*I*f you were to imagine what an abbey looked like, you may well conjure up something like this Tudor Gothic monastery, which rises from farmland in the serene lines of a medieval cathedral. Bell towers, windows etched in granite, and a cloister walk suggest that you are about to have a classic retreat experience. Indeed you will—if that's your wish. You've come to a place blessed, so far, with a relaxed setting that emphasizes solitude and private rooms (many retreat places elsewhere are booked months out, but there is good availability here).

In a few years, the abbey experience will include more amenities. An ambitious project is on track to build, by mid-decade, a modern retreat/conference center on a stunning vista about 20 miles away. Monks will probably be assigned to lead organized retreats. (The present, old-style offering is expected to remain open, too.)

Until modernizing takes hold, you are here pretty much on your own—a rather wonderful alternative to the tight organization of many retreat places. You may also come with a group or bring your own retreat master for a personal, directed retreat.

Your setting is a thoroughly lovely, old-fashioned complex that smells of old schoolhouses and fragrant wood. Accommodations are no-nonsense twin bed-and-sink rooms. These modest getaways with their cozy faded spreads and well-used furniture are not known as "cells" for nothing. But the abbey offers enough interesting sidelights that you won't stay in your cell for long. Wide grounds and pathways invite wandering meditations, including a stroll

Location: In the center of Cañon City, 80 miles southwest of Colorado Springs.

Description: Home to monks of the Order of St. Benedict, with overnight retreat accommodations.

Guest Profile: All welcome.

Spiritual Experience: Many opportunities for solitude and private, individual retreats.

How to get there: The abbey is easily visible at the eastern edge of Cañon City on the north side of Highway 50, the main road leading into and out of town.

into a secluded oak grove. If the urge to shop takes over, there's a modern and well-stocked religious gift store. If that urge is followed by the urge for a restaurant meal, you're in luck there, too, as you're less than a five-minute walk on the frontage road to a popular hotel restaurant.

What's more, in the monastery basement is a wonderful Indian museum, where artifacts and spiritual heritage are respected and lovingly cared for. Ask for a guided tour. One section includes a display of ancient boulders covered with Indian writing and art, saved from the bulldozer's jaws during a development project.

The abbey is located at the bustling edge of Cañon City, so expect to hear some traffic sounds from the adjacent highway and to be in sight of various buildings, including the edge of a car dealership. But look higher and take in the Wet Mountain range. Smack in front of you is the Sleeping Indian, a giant natural wonder visibly outlined by the crest of the mountain.

You will share your spiritual experience with about two dozen cloistered Benedictine monks. Their order came to Cañon City in 1924 and built this lovely complex, which is now on the National Register of Historic Places. The monks follow the 1,400-year-old rule of St. Benedict. Luckily for outsiders, St. Benedict decreed that rule 54 was to offer hospitality to guests. So while the monks spend much of their day in cloistered prayer and their daily activities, they invite regular interaction in the chapel.

Pedestals bearing full-size statues of the 12 apostles ring this airy, traditional haven. A local monk designed the altar and tabernacle. The eerily beautiful center crucifix, which seems suspended in mid-air, was made in Germany and donated in 1961. It used to hang in a student dorm, of all places, until it broke; then it lay in storage until 1992. You'll applaud its restoration.

Guests may gather here every day, beginning at 6 a.m. for morning prayer, for a 7 a.m. Mass, and for regular communal prayers throughout the day, ending at 7 p.m. Schedules may change, so be sure to confirm times.

An interesting sidelight to your abbey experience is the chance to join the monks for meals in their own dining "refectory." As you take in the scene—with the long, oaken tables and tall windows—you'll think you stumbled into a dining hall at an old English boys' school. This one is charmingly quirky: On one side is an old library with towering stacks, a tropical fish tank, and a chat area with overstuffed easy chairs.

This perk is available only when guest numbers are light. You must maintain complete silence at breakfast. Dinner is spent in silence listening to spiritual readings. Lunch is open to chats.

49. Horn Creek Retreat and Conference Center

6758 County Road 130
Westcliffe, CO 81252
719-783-2205
www.horncreek.org

This big, sprawling, resort-quality retreat center has something for everyone. Families will appreciate the opportunities to gather in cozy lodges and on well-maintained campus areas dotted with ponderosa pines. Kids will appreciate activities ranging from a gleaming bowling alley to a full gymnasium. There's a racquetball court, an indoor rock-climbing wall, and horseback riding. The water slide is so long and deliciously slithery it would turn heads in a first-class amusement park. For the energetic of all ages there's the chance for rafting, train rides to the nearby Royal Gorge, and hikes up Horn Peak, which towers just above the campsite.

For conference-goers, there is a state-of-the-art auditorium and meeting rooms large enough to accommodate church-sized crowds.

The constant at this year-round resort is that everybody should feel comfortable expressing interdenominational, evangelical Christianity. The camp was founded in the early 1950s by two ministers who dreamed of a Christian family camp in this part of Colorado. It opened in 1955 with a dozen kids and now serves 16,000 guests a year.

The lodging areas are divided into three campuses, an organizational tactic that allows many groups to meet here at the same time. The rustic lodges are lashed with stalwart beams and Paul Bunyan–sized fireplaces. Imagine a frosty winter night; you're curled up in a central fellowship area where the scent of a crackling fire and pine needles fills the cathedral ceilings. You and your better half contemplate a dip in the hot tub while Junior skitters across the broad-beamed upper balcony before your eyes, heading for your family-style bedroom down the hall.

Summertime is devoted mostly to families and individuals. The staff-planned activities range from square dancing and skits to talks by well-known Christian motivational speakers. During fall, winter, and spring, Horn Creek concentrates on Christian groups who provide their own staff and programs. That's also the time for organized conferences, which include couples' and singles' retreats and separate retreats for women and men. There are also retreats and "spiritual revival" conferences, which defy categories. In 2000, for example, the resort hosted Thanksgiving Week and Snow Camp. For a sense of the atmosphere, eavesdrop on how the retreat advertises for staff on its website: The staff is composed of about 40 "select Christian young people… expected to reflect Christ in all they do and say." The site adds that "Service at Horn Creek is service for Jesus Christ, and thus is a special privilege and responsibility that will long be remembered." Given the retreat's array of programming, multi-dimensional grounds, and robust list of activities, the memories are likely to stick with the guests, too.

Location: About 80 miles southwest of Colorado Springs.

Description: An interdenominational organization committed to providing Christian-based youth camps, family retreats, and group conferences.

Guest Profile: Adults, youth, singles.

Spiritual Experience: High-energy camp with many areas for solitude and getaways.

How to get there: From Highway 69 about 3 miles south of Westcliffe, turn west onto County Road 140 (Schoolfield Road; the sign is the size of a residential street sign, so watch carefully). You'll know you're close to 140 when you see signs for a landfill and Rosita Road. (From the intersection with 140, you're a total of 6.3 miles from Horn Creek.) Drive straight toward the mountains, for almost 2 miles. At Road 129 go left. Follow almost 2 miles to the intersection with Road 130/Horn Road; there is a sign for Horn Creek, pointing right. Drive 2.3 miles on this good combination paved/dirt road to the camp's arched entranceway.

50. JCC Ranch Camp

c/o Jewish Community Center
350 South Dahlia Street
Denver, CO 80246
303-316-6384
www.ranchcamp.org

*I*n the 19th century, this rugged ranch site was a stagecoach stop. In 1953, the Jewish Community Center bought the 400 acres and opened Colorado's only supervised kosher summer ranch for kids. The ranch maintains separate cooking and serving of food groups as prescribed by Jewish law. Meanwhile, kosher-style meals, a more relaxed designation, are observed at Camp Shwayder (see page 239). For nine weeks every summer, kids have a rip-roaring good time as they hike, camp, horseback ride, scale mountains—and learn about Jewish history and heritage.

JCC Ranch offers three lengths of stay, depending on age and inclination. The options include an 11-day wilderness trek and a Native American exchange in New Mexico. Older kids can learn technical climbing and leadership training. The vigorous stays—12 or 19 days, or a full month—take place in a rugged ranch that is literally sitting on top of a petrified forest, says director Juli Kramer.

The camp is dotted with cabins outfitted with bunk beds. An outdoor pavilion and a stage, called Eddie's Corner, form part of the complex, which overlooks the lovely tumble of plains and forested hills known as the Black Forest. The sheltered outdoor sites are the settings for some of the ranch's most meaningful moments, such as Friday night candlelight services and the morning Sabbath prayers on Saturday.

The camp welcomes all, and Jewish kids from every branch—reform, conservative, traditional, or reconstructionist—would feel comfortable here. Only the strictly Orthodox, who maintain separations between the genders, would find the accommodations difficult. Boys and girls have cabins in separate areas of the camp but mingle freely during outings, entertainment, and prayer services. A Judaic coordinator—sometimes a rabbi, always someone with expertise in Jewish history and practices—is a permanent member of the staff.

No one planned it this way, but year in, year out, about 20 percent of the youth who come here are non-Jewish. It's a great way to learn about another religion, says Kramer, and the idea is to make them feel comfortable while including them in all the activities and Jewish observances.

Location: Just outside Elbert, about 30 miles from Colorado Springs in the Black Forest area of the Front Range.

Description: A kosher summer camp designed to connect youth to the environment and expose them to Jewish ethics and Western-Judaic values.

Guest Profile: About 80 percent are Jewish youth, 7 to 15 years of age, of all denominations from reform to conservative and traditional. The rest are non-Jewish youth whose families want to give them an opportunity to learn more about another religion.

Spiritual Experience: A highly interactive camp with many sports available. Youth take part in weekly Shabbat (Sabbath) services, which begin after sundown on Fridays. There are traditional Jewish blessings before meals, Torah study on Saturdays, and evening entertainment and projects, such as skits, designed to promote understanding of the Torah and Jewish practices.

How to get there: From Denver, take I-25 to the Founders Parkway (Exit 184). Go east to Highway 86, and continue on 86 past Franktown to Elizabeth. (From Colorado Springs, take Exit 182, the exit for Franktown and Highway 86.) This is a 16-mile drive through horse country and ranchland. From the town of Elizabeth, continue past the stoplight 7 miles and look for Elbert Road, which is next to the entrance sign for the town of Kiowa. Go south on Elbert 10 miles to the town of Elbert. The camp is 3 miles beyond the town's center, past the Boy Scout ranch and Peaceful Valley. Look for the sign on the right side of the highway, with an archway leading to the camp.

51. Mercy Center

520 West Buena Ventura Street
Colorado Springs, CO 80907
719-633-2302
Fax: 719-633-1031
E-mail: info@mercycenter.com
www.mercycenter.com

*G*uests recharge their spiritual batteries in this converted gas station, now dressed up as a charming, two-story pink stucco. The Rev. Bill Jarema, a Catholic priest, founded the center in 1988. A guest with a taste for whimsy might call this a "full-service" healing center—a repair shop for the body, mind, and spirit.

Counselors, as well as guests, cut across all religious and mental health traditions. Staff ranges from priests to psychotherapists, massage therapists, and dream interpreters. Guiding principles include the philosophy of Carl Jung, the father of 20th-century analytical psychology whose ideas popularized concepts such as dreamwork, the collective unconscious, and group therapy. His work encouraged further explor-ation into Eastern religions and astrology. Guests at Mercy Center begin their stay by taking part in Jungian mandala assessment, a tool that brings issues to conscious awareness by plumbing the unconscious mind. That's done in either a group or individual setting, says Tim Fogle, director.

While its rules are relaxed—there's no minimum stay, and a few guests have been here a year or more—all guests must sign up for a personal assessment of their healing needs. Those needs may be as mild as a longing for a weekend spiritual getaway or as harrowing as a broken relationship, domestic abuse, or a crisis in one's vocation. The center specializes in guiding people through midlife transitions and helping

Location: Colorado Springs.

Description: A retreat house specializing in "healing the whole person."

Guest Profile: All interested in combining spiritual retreat with a variety of techniques that include psychotherapy, therapeutic touch, and dreamwork.

Spiritual Experience: Guests may seek their own level of solitude, but also take part in a personalized healing program, which may include a directed retreat and/or other psychotherapeutic and spiritual programs.

How to get there: In Colorado Springs, take the Uintah exit off I-25 and head west one block to Walnut Street. Turn right (north) and go three blocks, at which point Walnut becomes Buena Ventura. Mercy Center is on the first corner.

priests, nuns, and those in religious life deal with challenges in their vocation.

You might say Mercy Center's atmosphere is as complex as one's own psyche. A cheerfully cluttered downstairs houses the offices and the main conference room, which is the gas station's former drive-in bay. Here, adults work with clay, watercolor and sand, weaving, and drawing to express their hidden potential. Upstairs are living quarters for about a dozen guests. The comfortable warren of bedrooms is flanked by a homey kitchen and dining area. The heart of the place is a cozy sitting room decorated in laid-back gray and egg-yolk yellow. Its ceiling is a soaring greenhouse window open to the sky.

Next to the main building is the newly renovated Chapel of the Exalted Cross. Although guests hail from many religious backgrounds, Catholic Mass is celebrated here daily. During Holy Week—the solemn week before Easter—everyone is asked to maintain a measure of silence.

Mercy Center has recently bought up several nearby ranch- and bungalow-style homes in this old, residential neighborhood. Guests may take a room in those homes or in the main building, and the staff is proud that no one has ever been turned away. The center is a stone's throw from the hurly-burly of I-25, but sound barriers keep the highway out of sight and mind. Guests are an easy, two-block stroll from the meditative beauty of Biedleman Environmental Center at Sonderman Park, a lovely preserve with pathways.

52. Ponderosa Retreat and Conference Center

15235 Furrow Road
Larkspur, CO 80118-5703
800-900-0884
www.visitponderosa.com

"Experience God at Ponderosa," says the brochure. And, it might add, come to God's country to do it. You won't have to go far, either, because Ponderosa is one of those camps that seem to be in the middle of the forest primeval, but actually it's less than a dozen freeway exits shy of Colorado Springs' downtown.

Located under the brows of Bald and True Mountains, Ponderosa makes the most of its backcountry setting. As Rockies go, the mountains are gentle for climbing, and the 670 acres—a former cattle ranch—offer pretty tramps through ponderosa pine and meadows that break out onto the Front Range. Part of your meditative hike leads to an area registered as a national heritage site because it contains a rare form of oat grass, says director Gary Sparrow. In the distance, Pikes Peak looms.

Location: About 30 miles equal distance between Denver and Colorado Springs, about 3 miles east of I-25.

Description: An activity-oriented camp geared to groups, families, and youth.

Guest Profile: Evangelical church groups and those seeking a Christian, Bible- and family-centered experience.

Spiritual Experience: Geared to activities and family-oriented events; sprawling backcountry grounds suited to hiking getaways.

How to get there: From I-25, take Exit 163 (County Line Road). Go east 1.8 miles to Furrow Road (County Road 57). You'll see a sign for the camp at that intersection. Go left and drive another 0.9 mile to the entrance.

There's horseback riding, hayrides, a challenge course, Frisbee golf, and volleyball. But what makes this camp tick is its commitment to providing a spiritual setting for Christian church groups and families. Summertime is devoted to kids and youth groups during the week and family reunions and adult retreats on weekends. From September to May, Ponderosa opens to church and nonprofit groups such as hospitals and schools as well as couples and those seeking a personal retreat.

Accommodations range from pleasantly rustic to resort quality. There are dormitory style rooms with bunk beds as well as deluxe suites with TVs, some cabins with full kitchens, and several hotel-quality rooms with their own baths. There's also RV space. The conference center, run by Colorado Southern Baptists, is updating a little every year by painting and adding new carpets. It hopes to soon add more to its year-round capacity of 350 (about 100 more during the summer).

You'll find a classic A-frame chapel with pews and, a short hike from the main camp, a very sweet stone chapel which guests often seek out for meditation. Prior to the 1960s, when this was a cattle ranch, the stone chapel was the "spring house" located over a natural spring. Perhaps 10 by 16 feet, the interior has simple folding chairs, a prayer bench, and a cross. Just beyond the chapel is a special prayer path, which contains prayer stations and meditation benches.

53. Templed Hills Camp and Retreat Center

1364 County Road 75
Woodland Park, CO 80863
719-687-9038 or 1-800-229-6955
E-mail: retreatinfo@templedhills.org
www.templedhills.org

"We're here for whomever the Lord sends us," says Art Rousseau, facilities manager. That relaxed and easygoing tone permeates this pretty camp. Log-framed paths meander into the rolling hills, past cabins and campfire circles. Through stands of ponderosa pine, guests can marvel at the forested tiers of the Rampart Range.

Sleeping accommodations range from private rooms to what the camp calls "four walls and a light bulb." (They throw in a cot, too.) There are also several lodges, including a handsome new lodge called Eagles Nest with 20 private rooms that sleeps up to 88. Meeting rooms are also available. If your spiritual needs are bigger than your bank account, you can bring your own food and use the cooking facilities. As for the program, the camp advertises "opportunities for peace and solitude" and invites guests to hike the mountain trails to find it.

Location: In the Pike National Forest, about 25 miles northwest from downtown Colorado Springs.

Description: A year-round retreat facility run by the United Methodist Church, with outdoor activities and a staff that practices a ministry of hospitality.

Guest Profile: Church groups of every denomination, nonprofit groups, family reunions. Day meetings welcome.

Spiritual Experience: Solitude available along streams and trails.

How to get there: From I-25 in Colorado Springs, take Highway 24 west (the Cimarron exit, with additional signs for Manitou Springs and Pikes Peak). Drive 19 miles to the center of the town of Woodland Park. Pass several stoplights in town, and look for the intersection with Highway 67. Drive north 4 miles and look on the left for the sign to the camp. Drive a short way up a dirt road.

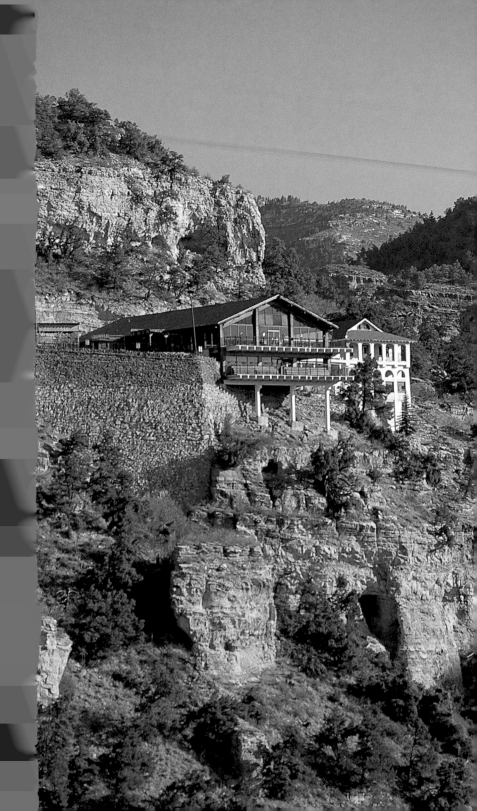

Sacred Places

Sacred sites are not for gawkers. Native Americans rightly resent having their ancient gathering places dismissed as an afternoon's tourist stop. Many of their sacred places in Colorado are off limits to the public. But the Southern Front Range offers guests a unique opportunity to explore sites "legally" and at the same time pay quiet tribute to their ancient spiritual meaning.

54. Cave of the Winds

A cave is a mysterious place, whether protected by a guardian spirit or a turnstile. Guests are in for a mind-gripping tour when they enter this hauntingly beautiful cave outside Colorado Springs, the largest on the Front Range. Much of its Native American heritage is shrouded in secrets, though one of its personality quirks—a virtual nonstop growling of the wind—was apparently considered as remarkable in ancient times as now. Apaches believed a great spirit of the winds resided in the cave, invisible except for its writhing formlessness: the stuff of whirlwinds, sand devils, and tornadoes, says Richard Rhinehart, author of *Colorado Caves.* In the early 1960s tribal descendants set down in writing much of the sacred significance of the caves, including the old belief that "only the bravest of the brave would ever go into the cave—and not very far," Rhinehart says.

Today, lines of tourists explore the cave through and through. Its popularity makes it very easy to find. From I-25, take the Manitou Springs/ Pikes Peak exit, which is Highway 24 west. Stay on 24—don't turn into town—and as you head west, look for the entrance sign just a few minutes' drive from town. For more information, call the Manitou Springs Chamber of Commerce at 800-642-2567 or check out the website at www.manitousprings.org.

55. Garden of the Gods

*B*oth an ancient tribal site and a natural cathedral, these ruddy spires continue to beckon the soul with the promise of peace and solitude. As you wander its winding trails, you can well imagine that this was a spot where ancient tribes gathered. "This is one of those places we know was home to the spirits," says Alden Naranjo, a Southern Ute who works as a historian and consultant on Native American issues. He mentions the "little people": spirits akin to leprechauns who were believed to live here. But Garden of the Gods was significant for other reasons, too. It appears to have been a natural intertribal meeting place for a meal; archaeologists have uncovered striking evidence of cooking hearths on the park grounds.

There was at one time also the troubling possibility that this tourist hotspot was a sacred site for burying the dead. In the early 1990s, city officials, preservationists, and Native American representatives sat down to develop a master plan to protect the sacred nature of this wondrous place. Gene Smith, cultural services supervisor for Garden of the Gods, recalls the setting: "We went in with a specific question: Were there Ute burials in the Garden of the Gods?" To the officials' relief, "they indicated this was not a place they would bury people." However, Smith said, it was clear from tribal testimony that this was "a place the Utes would come to visit, for several reasons."

For one thing, the natural red spires offered both heat-retaining faculties and wind-cutting coziness. That created a balmy climate, even in the sharpest winter blast—an ideal natural retreat. What's more, the area was adjacent to an ancient site of healing mineral waters. "Manitou Springs was a place where they would lay down their arms," Smith says. "Enemies would be at peace with one another at the springs. The springs is probably a site that comes closest to that word 'sacred.'"

Just as guests are welcome today to walk the trails in Garden of the Gods, they may also seek out the springs revered by native tribes. Note, though, that these are not hot springs, but fonts of naturally carbonated water prized for its mineral properties. You may collect the water free at more than a half-dozen locations throughout the town of Manitou Springs. Almost any resident or shopkeeper can point out the nearest fountain, or you can stop for a map at the Chamber of Commerce office, 354 Manitou Avenue.

To honor its ancient past, Garden of the Gods was reconfigured in the mid-1990s based on the master plan and Native American consultations. The rustic gift shop and restaurant were moved from the heart of the needling spires to the edge of the property. After decades of putting tourists first, Garden of the Gods has recaptured more of the pristine and meditative beauty that drew Native Americans here for centuries.

Visitors may easily find this jewel of the Colorado Springs city park system by taking the Garden of the Gods exit off I-25 and following the signs west several miles. For more information, contact the Manitou Springs Chamber of Commerce at 1-800-642-2567 or access their website, www.manitousprings.org.

56. Pikes Peak

"**I**t was considered the center of the world. It was like their Mount Sinai," Ute historian Alden Naranjo says of his tribe's reverence for Pikes Peak. Guests may go to the top of this dramatic Fourteener by hiking or riding a train that leaves regularly from the station in Manitou Springs. For centuries, tribal bands sought out this graceful queen of the plains, which rises 1.5 miles higher than any of its immediate surroundings. For Utes, the massif, which they called Sun Mountain, was an excellent logistical help: "Any direction they went, they could keep it in view," says Naranjo. The peak's importance was fixed by the belief that life began here. "What you white men call 'medicine men' went up there," he adds. "They would go there like you make pilgrimages to Rome or the Wailing Wall."

For modern pilgrims, the transport is a cog-rail train that runs about eight times a day from roughly Memorial Day to Labor Day and a little beyond, depending on the weather. Reserve 3 hours and 20 minutes for the train trip alone, which includes a half-hour on the summit. And however counterintuitive it may strike you, be sure to bring a warm weather jacket along. Even in sweltering July, it's frosty and windy at 14,110 feet above sea level.

To get there, take the Manitou Springs/Pikes Peak exit off I-25 and follow the signs into town. Look for Ruxton Avenue, which angles off the town's main drag. Take Ruxton up the hill a few blocks until you come to the depot. For more information, contact the Manitou Springs Chamber of Commerce at 1-800-642-2567 or www.manitousprings.org.

Other Spiritual Destinations

Bear Trap Ranch nestled among the pines.

Bear Trap Ranch

8655 Old Stage Road, Colorado Springs, CO 80906; 719-632-0740
(www.ivcf.org/beartrap): Located 8 miles southwest of Colorado Springs in
mountainous terrain at 9,100 feet elevation in the Pike National Forest. (Four-wheel
drive necessary during winter.) One of four national training centers for the
InterVarsity Christian Fellowship and site of the famous "Wrangler's Breakfast," this
ranch serves small board meetings, family-oriented events, and retreats for up to
100 guests.

Colorado Camp Cherith

30150 Highway 67, Woodland Park, CO 80863; 970-353-3170: Year-round
Bible- and Christ-centered outdoor program for youth.

Colorado Christian Camp

P.O. Box 2034, Monument, CO 80132; 719-488-0855: A camp specializing in ice hockey programs.

Eagle Lake Camp

P.O. Box 6000, Colorado Springs, CO 80934; 719-472-1260:
"To inspire Christ-centered love and commitment through counselor relationships."
A year-round adventure and outdoor camp for youth and families, with special outreach to economically disadvantaged guests.

Golden Bell Conference Center

380 County Road 512, Divide, CO 80814; 719-687-9561: A year-round center for youth, families, and adults that specializes in inner-city youth, senior citizens, home schoolers, and singles.

Lutheran Valley Retreat

P.O. Box 9042, Woodland Park, CO 80866; 719-687-3560: A year-round outdoors ministry for youth and families.

Quaker Ridge Camp

30150 North Highway 67, Woodland Park, CO 80863; 719-687-9012: For adults and youth, with special outreach to intercultural groups and singles.

Quaker Ridge Christian Camp and Conference Center has been a retreat of the Society of Friends, also known as the Quakers, since 1949.

Above: Rockcleft, a secluded camp offering Bible study and private retreats, is administered by the Central Church of Christ, Wichita.

Rockcleft

P.O. Box 326, Cascade, CO 80819; 719-684-9551: Located off Highway 24 about 15 miles west of Colorado Springs. Open mid-May to mid-October; youth groups dominate mid-July to mid-August. Directors hope to build up clientele during other times and seek people for single and private retreats with a Christian emphasis for prayer, meditation, and small-group Bible study. Very secluded and heavily forested at 8,600 feet elevation. Five cabins available.

Rocky Mountain Mennonite Camp

709 County Road 62, Divide, CO 80814; 719-687-9506: A camp for families, youth, adults, and couples.

Upon the Rock Wilderness Retreats

7437 North 95th Street, Longmont, CO 80501; 303-652-0717: Christian adventure, hiking, and backcountry programs in southern Colorado.

The InterVarsity Christian Fellowship's Bear Trap Ranch is a converted dude ranch.

Region Five:
Crestone and the San Luis Valley

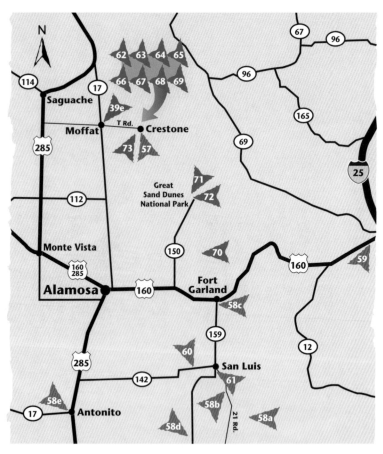

Listing information for 39e above is on p.112.

*S*et in the trough of a huge granite wave, Crestone looks as vulnerable as a dot on a map. Which, in a way, it is. Just over its shoulder to the east, the Sangre de Cristo Range looks like one long breaker about to hurl itself over the town's handful of stores and a populace in the hundreds.

For eons, though, the mountain wave has been frozen in place.

And Crestone? Though a speck in size, in these parts it's the real mover and shaker. In the last decades of the 20th century it moved steadily to solidify its reputation as "the largest intentional interfaith ecumenical community in North America." That's the long-range goal of Hanne and Maurice Strong. You need to know those two names to understand why—if you desire to plunge into Eastern spirituality, explore the New Age, or get within a few degrees' separation of an Arab king (see Ziggurat, page 194)—someday you'll probably be headed for Crestone.

Of course, seekers and pioneers have always pursued their faith and dreams into the San Luis Valley. Many Native American tribes considered it the most sacred place on the planet. When Spanish conquistadors moved up from Mexico, they brought the Catholic faith, which to this day has stamped the southern San Luis Valley region with its own distinctive religious personality. (For one destination among an array of interesting spiritual sites, drive south from Alamosa about 25 miles on Highway 285 to the town of Conejos, where Our Lady of Guadalupe Church is revered as the site of the oldest parish in Colorado.)

Spiritual pilgrims still come to the San Luis Valley to worship at San Acacio, a 150-year-old Catholic pioneer parish bound by a miracle, or to walk along a trail dedicated to a magnificent, life-sized Stations of the Cross, to name just two sanctuaries listed here. The stations, a centuries-old Catholic tradition, depicts Christ's walk to Calvary. Located in the town of San Luis and completed in the mid-1990s, the stations already draws people of all religious traditions from around the country.

The Divine Mother Temple at Haidakhandi Ashram in Crestone is a site for devotional practices in the Hindu tradition.

But the world is beating a path to Crestone today, thanks, in large part, to the influence of an international power-couple named Strong. Since the 1970s Hanne and Maurice Strong have been developing Crestone—literally and figuratively—as a peaceful crossroads for both ancient religions and New Age sensibilities, both mystical and environmental. Maurice is a Canadian businessman who, in a 1978 land transaction, bought up the vast plains east of Crestone known as the Baca. Among its many treasures, one of the largest fresh-water aquifers in the world nestles under its surface.

Inspired by both new-world and environmentalist ideals (Maurice was a reckoning force behind the 1992 Earth Summit in Rio de Janeiro), the Strongs have set many dreams to percolating in the San Luis Valley. An early idea was to put the Aspen Institute for Humanistic Studies on the land. But the area proved too remote for regular visits from such notables as Henry Kissinger or PBS personality Bill Moyers, according to author Marci McDonald in a 1994 profile of the Strongs. If the Aspen Institute didn't last here, perhaps another kind of settlement would—and all because the Strongs sensed that something even more divine than water seethes beneath Crestone. McDonald writes that on a hiking trip during one institute visit, Moyers saw a bush burst mysteriously into flame. He still discusses the experience with Hanne, according to the article, and treasures it as the only mystical experience he has ever had.

Hanne sensed the spiritual undercurrents too. In her elegantly rustic backyard overlooking the Baca plains, Strong, a native of Denmark, still lights up as she tells a visitor about the mysterious message she received in 1978, the year she came to her wilderness address.

One day an elderly local mystic named Glenn Anderson arrived at her door with a stark greeting: "So, you've finally come." Anderson was convinced that Hanne Strong was the force meant to bring the world's religions together in one safe place, protected from worldwide cataclysm. "This vision of all the religions of the world coming together—this was the vision of Crazy Horse," says Strong, referring to the great Lakota warrior of the plains. "The purpose of this place is to bring forth a new generation of children, a new civilization of people who can live in harmony with the earth, each other, and everything that is living."

So the Strongs began. Already in place was $30 million worth of infrastructure, including roads and utilities, that a previous developer had installed for a failed retirement village. The couple donated land to get the first three spiritual settlements going. (All three are in these pages: the Nada Hermitage, the Haidakhandi Universal Ashram, and the Sri Aurobindo Learning Center.) In 1988 the Strongs established the Manitou Foundation, a private nonprofit foundation, to expand their original plan. Supported by the foundation and the Manitou Institute, a public charity that offers land grants, the Baca Grande subdivision has a continuously growing array of spiritual retreat centers, many of which are detailed here as well.

With its meandering streets, clean-lined elegance, and windows soaring to the sky, the Baca Grande looks like a cozy neighborhood in southern California. If you're here as a guest, your destination may be an easy drive off the main street, called Camino Baca Grande, or an adven-turous plunge into backcountry dirt roads that take some patience to navigate. Be fore-warned that this relaxed, rural layout (a mix of nicely paved streets, gravel roads, and maverick signage) makes directions subjective and, yes, often maddening to the newcomer. While you'll encounter many residents eager to help you find your way around this unique part of the world, you may just as easily run across long-timers who are reluctant to encourage curiosity seekers barreling around their lovely development.

So, if that next turn looks confusing, you may have to risk making new friends by appealing for help from nearby neighbors.

In any case, Crestone apparently has a powerful effect on both visitors and settlers. Some people come intending to buy land and settle, but can't bear the psychic energy and have to leave, says Hanne Strong. Others make their way here and then can't leave, because of the same magnetic draw. "The power of this land is mind boggling," she says. "You come within a hundred miles and begin to feel it. It's so pure, so powerful—a female, soft energy, not a hard male energy." She believes it's precisely these mystic properties that make this such a good place for retreat. "When you come here, you have to deal with your problem. You have to face it."

You can find out for yourself if she's right.

Sanctuaries

57. Little Shepherd in the Hills Episcopal Church

Rev. John Huffman, pastor
Crestone, CO 81131
719-539-4562

*O*nly here, in what is arguably the American capital of Eastern spirituality, could this sight look exotic: Set back meekly into a wildflower-strewn lot, in the heart of Crestone, is an old log church. A sign proclaims it to be Little Shepherd in the Hills Episcopal Church. It's been a working church for 60 years, and a century ago it was Eva Tooker's log home, according to *An Illustrated Guide to the Significant Attractions of the Crestone/Baca Area* by local restaurateur Lynda Kucin. In 1949 Alfred and Helen Collins turned it into a church for the Christian community.

After the Eastern-style spirituality and opulence, a visitor might find this kind of sacred place a change of pace for an impromptu prayer or Bible reading. Tiptoe across the lawn and peek in the window. You'll be treated to a lovely, homespun scene, like a moment frozen in 19th-century time—a little country kirk waiting for worshipers to arrive: A handsome, handcarved organ sits against one wall. Dark blue bench pews offer seats for 30. The altar, dressed for service, is adorned with gleaming candlesticks and a cross. A huge, beribboned prayer book lies open and ready for reading.

Location: The center of the town of Crestone.

Description: A tiny mission church with a rich history.

Guest Profile: Explorers of the sacred.

Spiritual Experience: Sunday services at 2:30 p.m. for Eucharist and evening prayer (as of early 2001).

How to get there: From Highway 17, drive to the town of Moffat. Look for a road marked "T" that heads east. (A Crestone sign is also nearby.) Go 12 miles, straight into the mountains, until the road forks. A left turn takes you into Crestone. The church is on the main street into town, set back from the road, on the left-hand side.

58. Penitente Brotherhood

Some Lenten rituals of the Penitente Brotherhood have drawn unwanted media attention to 400-year-old practices, but traditional worships and processionals continue to this day. Photo courtesy of Colorado Historical Society.

They look so modest. Yet 400 years of history holds up these prayer halls that dot southern Colorado. For centuries, they kept alive the Catholic faith in the New World.

To this day, members of an ancient Catholic lay organization called the Penitente Brotherhood come to moradas (prayer chapels) to pray and praise God, especially during the Lenten season. They also routinely pool their time and resources for community members in need. Sadly, the number of moradas in southern Colorado is fragile. Many modern spiritual seekers, apparently, find it difficult to relate to the brotherhood's intensely prayerful traditions and emphasis on doing penance for sins (thus the name "penitente").

Members are eager, however, to pass along their heritage and welcome requests for private tours. Moradas, simple rooms with an altar, pews, and Stations of the Cross on the walls, are a good place to come and reflect on the ordeals some believers have endured in order to hold fast to their faith.

The Penitentes, a group of lay men, organized in 1599. (Today, women are included as well.) Their purpose? To keep alive the Catholic faith that had only recently arrived from Europe. Spanish friars, who knew all too well that their missionary efforts could reach only so far into vast, uncharted North America, began the lay group to spread the faith where they could not. Their efforts meant that a century before George Washington was president, the Penitentes had already taken up the task of gathering fellow Catholics to say the rosary, bury the dead, and gather for Sunday worship, though they remained bereft of Mass unless a priest came. The Penitentes are still known for their deep spirituality during the Lenten season, when Christians traditionally intensify prayer, fasting, and works of mercy as a way to prepare for the observance on Good Friday of Jesus Christ's death and of His resurrection on Easter Sunday.

Until well into the 20th century, Penitentes were also known for something else: their often severe penances, especially during Lent, which included walking to church on their knees and self-flagellation (whipping one's back with a stout strap). However, the age of cameras and videotape has pretty much put a stop to those public practices, says Vernal Martinez. When shown in photographs and on television, such spiritual severity became sensationalized and invited misunderstandings and mockery, thus only harming the cause of faith.

Lent is still a wonderful time to join the Penitentes in their worship. On Ash Wednesday, the beginning of Lent, members gather in the moradas for their annual organizational meeting. On Fridays during Lent they recite the traditional Stations of the Cross. Holy Week, the solemn final week of Lent, is marked by many Penitente rituals and worships, including processionals through the towns. That week the moradas are open more often than not, as members gather until late at night to pray the rosary, the Stations of the Cross, and other Lenten prayers.

There are now just several dozen members in Colorado, though the brotherhood is thriving in New Mexico. Members would like to attract new blood to their ancient heritage. After all, not many groups can celebrate what the Penitente Brotherhood celebrated in 1999: their 400th anniversary.

Location: The brotherhood maintains about a half-dozen moradas, or prayer chapels, throughout the southern San Luis Valley in the towns of San Francisco (**58a**), San Pedro (**58b**), Fort Garland (**58c**), Garcia (**58d**), and Antonito (**58e**).

Description: The Penitentes use moradas for their centuries-old Catholic devotions.

Guest Profile: Those interested in learning more about this 400-year-old Hispanic tradition are welcome to make an appointment to see one of the moradas, which are kept locked.

Spiritual Experience: A touching opportunity for modern seekers to connect with traditional spiritual devotion as well as a part of America's heritage.

How to get there: Your first step on this journey is best made via telephone. Moradas are scattered through several small towns in the valley, each under the auspices of different brotherhood members who are very protective of these sacred places of prayer. Unless you make direct contact with a member, you probably can't get inside these chapels. Vernal Martinez, head of the morada near Antonito, which is on Highway 285 near the New Mexico line, welcomes calls at 719-376-5926. Jose F. Vigil and his wife, Lucy, also oversee moradas in the valley; they welcome calls at 719-376-5252. You'll find helpful advice from the Sangre de Cristo Parish in San Luis, site of the famous Stations of the Cross (see page 168); call the office at 719-672-3685.

59. The People's Shrine

Location: Just west of Walsenburg.

Description: A nameless shrine.

Guest Profile: Curious travelers.

Spiritual Experience: Sweetly moving.

How to get there: The shrine is about 6 miles west of Walsenburg's main street on the north side of Highway 160. You'll be almost on top of it when you come to a highway marker identifying the Spanish Peaks and, underneath, the peaks' Indian name, Huajatolla.

Don't let roaring traffic speed you, unknowingly, past this homely yet touching shrine. On the side of busy Highway 160, under the cover of a massive natural stone altar in Colorado's distinctive, iron-red sandstone, is a spontaneous gesture of faith built by ordinary people. The twin Spanish Peaks rise gracefully in solitary splendor off the plains and appear directly opposite this little shrine. But so striking is the orange rock formation that once you know it's there, it will be difficult to miss.

In the eerily perfect stone recesses, nameless believers have placed statues of the Blessed Virgin and saints, surrounded by flowers and candles. But that's only the beginning of the spiritual decorations adorning these rock shelves, which are perhaps 15 feet high and span 30 paces from end to end. In bulges and tiny caves, people have strung rosaries and beadwork and ribbons. Barbed wire protects the wide "altar" area (though there's an easy place to duck under if, say, you wished to leave your own spiritual memento). The cruel-looking metal thorns are softened by hundreds of items strung through them: children's toys, twigs braided into crosses, baby sneakers, and medals. The largest item—a sturdy wooden cross about seven feet tall—offers a hint, perhaps, of why this shrine began. Burned into its beams are the names Joe G. and Manuelita Gonzales, and fastened to the outstretched limbs are heartrending personal items: broken eyeglasses, an old striped T-shirt, a rosary, and a large, homemade red paper heart.

60. San Acacio Parish

Sangre de Cristo Parish
P.O. Box 326
San Luis, CO 81152
719-672-3685

Location: East of San Acacio, 45 miles from Alamosa and 5 miles west of San Luis.

Description: An adobe church resting on a site that dates back to the mid-1800s.

Guest Profile: All welcome.

Spiritual Experience: A place to pause and reflect. Catholic Masses are held at 6 p.m. on the third Sunday of every month (as of 2001).

How to get there: From San Luis on Highway 159, take Highway 142 west about 5 miles. (Note: On some maps, "San Acacio Viejo" may appear. This church is in the vicinity of "old San Acacio," not of the modern town, which is about 3 miles farther west.) Watch for a row of houses on your left and a dirt road that should be marked as County Road 15. Turn south, and drive about a mile until you see the church.

*W*hile the present church dates from the mid-20th century, local legend insists it stands on the site of a miracle. The story's edges have been softened and burnished by time, but here's how the local residents tell it to this day, as circulated in a written history by Maclovio C. Martinez: In the mid-1800s a band of local families, who hailed from Spanish settlements in northern New Mexico, were working in the fields when word came of an Indian war party cresting the main southern elevation near the site (believed to be where the Sanchez Canal runs today). Woefully inadequate in the fighting department, the settlers knelt and prayed for the intercession of someone who did have military muscle: a third-century saint called Acacius, long revered as a Roman centurion who converted to Christianity and was martyred for his faith. They asked Acacius to beg God to spare them from bloodshed. Nevertheless, the war party headed toward them at full gallop. All seemed lost—when, suddenly, the war party stopped. The settlers saw them look up into the sky, pointing their spears and bows upward. Then the entire mass of warriors turned and inexplicably galloped away.

Much later, an elderly Indian woman who joined the Spanish-speaking settlement said she had information about the mysterious doings of that day. According to her written account, circulated by Martinez, the Indian braves reported that, as they headed for the pioneer settlement, they looked up and saw in the sky the image of a great warrior prepared to defend the settlers. "The image so startled them with its power that they pulled up and retreated, never to return," the account states.

In thanksgiving, the settlers named the area after the long-ago Roman centurian who they believe protected them. Indeed, it would be modern life, not war parties, that ultimately would cause the town to lose many of its 300 residents after World War II. As Martinez poignantly puts it, "When the young men in San Acacio were called to active duty to serve their country, they left the peaceful village to eventually see Japan, the Pacific and Europe. Small wonder that when these veterans returned to this quiet village, they were unafraid to move on in search of a future where jobs were to be found." Yet how many cities, job-rich as they may be, could say they were founded on a miracle?

61. San Luis Stations of the Cross

Sangre de Cristo Parish
P.O. Box 326
San Luis, CO 81152
719-672-3685

There may well be no site in North America that brings Christians closer to the reality of Jesus Christ's walk to Calvary than this rock-strewn hillside. Rising from the main street of this picturesque little southwestern town—one of Colorado's oldest—the hillside is studded with life-sized bronze statues re-creating Christ's walk to crucifixion 2,000 years ago. Known most commonly in the Catholic faith as Stations of the Cross, the lifelike figures depict each stage of Christ's agonizing journey.

As is tradition, the last station is a triumphant depiction of Christ rising from the dead, which here culminates in a stunning southwestern-style chapel at the crest of the hill. The view is as inspiring as the walk, offering nearly 360 degrees of Colorado's snow-capped skyscrapers. The stations' powerfully rendered human figures are taken from actual acquaintances and friends, says the sculptor, Huberto Maestas, who lives in town. They are all here: the suffering Jesus, the brutal guards, the onlookers, and Mary, Christ's mother. As you follow the path upwards you become part of the 2,000-year-old scene, too —a powerful, unusual perspective that creates a hush among even the longest lines of tourists. No wonder people of every faith have made this a beloved spot, especially during Lent and Easter.

Location: San Luis, in the heart of the San Luis Valley.

Description: An outdoor replica of Christ's walk to Calvary, sculpted in life-sized dimensions.

Guest Profile: All welcome.

Spiritual Experience: Intense, personal, and spiritually challenging, the San Luis Stations of the Cross has drawn people from all over the country.

How to get there: From Walsenburg, take Highway 160 west to Fort Garland. Take Highway 159 south 16 miles into San Luis.

There is also a sense of mystery here: that this small, homespun town, with its modest resources, far-from-flashy tourist attractions, could create such an elegantly simple and sacred place that has captured so many hearts. A group of devout Catholic businesspeople and the Knights of Columbus developed the idea and began raising money. One of their first coups, in addition to acquiring the steep, scrubby hill across from the Sangre de Cristo Parish Church, was enlisting the genius of Maestas, who still has his studio in town, located on Main Street almost adjacent to Station Hill. Not the least of this place's enchanting surprises is that visitors may drop in at Maestas' studio to browse through his sculptures and artwork.

Before you leave, be sure to stop in at the Sangre de Cristo Parish Church, located directly across the street from Station Hill. It's a unique example of French adobe architecture. The interior, lovingly renovated, shimmers with old wood and the original, noble-faced statues of the 19th century. Catholic Masses are celebrated here on Saturdays and Sundays. Call the church for times.

The town, too, is well worth a stroll. Despite a steady stream of visitors, San Luis has kept the unpretentious wholesomeness of a small town. Yet it also has several restaurants and ice cream parlor/gift shops where you can buy religious statues, jewelry, rosaries, and postcards. You may want to buy some postcards of the powerfully rendered sculptures— among other reasons, because this is a spiritual site, not a place to be snapping photographs. What's more, without postcards you may find it difficult to describe the intensity of the place to folks back home.

Retreats

62. Crestone Mountain Zen Center

P.O. Box 130
Crestone, CO 81131
719-256-4692

Location: Baca Grande subdivision, adjacent to Crestone.

Description: A Buddhist monastery available for serious retreats and study.

Guest Profile: Retreatants must be serious practitioners of Buddhist meditation. Not open for casual retreats.

Spiritual Experience: Intense and focused.

How to get there: Follow the main road in the Baca Grande to the end of the pavement. Turn right onto Camino Real, the road locals call "Two Trees." You will begin seeing yellow signs to the Haidakhandi Ashram. Follow the signs until, when you get to the top of Spanish Creek Trail, they indicate that the ashram is to the left. Turn right to get to the Zen Center, and follow until you reach the distinctive dwelling.

*R*igorous Zen Buddhist training marks this centerpiece of the Crestone experience. It's so rigorous that this retreat haven, under the leadership of Richard Baker-roshi, declined to open its doors for an interview. The center, a spokesman explains, only takes retreatants who are serious students of the Zen discipline, which follows the lineage of Shunryu Suzuki-roshi. They tell us they'd prefer to work with the spiritually committed rather than with spiritual dilettantes (sorry, dear reader) who may stumble upon them while flipping idly through the pages of a guidebook. Still, the Zen Center is invariably one of the first retreat centers mentioned by area residents, and it is prominently displayed in local guidebooks and business directories. It is open to visitors during summer months, and serious students take part in year-round training. The center is visually arresting and instantly recognized by its interwoven wood roof, which resembles an overturned basket.

63. Eagle's Nest Sanctuary

P.O. Box 369
888 Pinecone Way
Crestone, CO 81131
719-256-4149 or 1-888-524-8627
E-mail: eaglesnest@amigo.net

*W*hen only a real Kahuna priest will do, come to this aerie and learn the spiritual wisdom of the Hawaiian Islands. Two Kahuna priests, Lono and Kaikelani ("Lani") Ho'ala, will be your guides. Lono's spiritual odyssey took him from boyhood in Colorado to a Benedictine monastery and then to the islands. Lani was born and raised in Edinburgh, Scotland. Together, they discovered answers to their life questions in the ancient wisdom of Huna.

The ancient belief system may be summed up in a sentence: "God is everything that is." Followers believe that Huna's ancient founders came from the stars more than 40,000 years ago to deliver this universal religion to humanity. Huna means "something that is secret" or, at a deeper level, "the sacred knowledge of that which is real." Lono was adopted by a family of Kahuna priests and ordained, then sent to the mainland to open a center and teach these principles. He says Eagle's Nest Sanctuary is the only center of its kind operating on the U.S. mainland.

Guests learn about Lono and Lani as they settle into their lovely home, which is something like stepping into a southern California "house beautiful" advertisement. Despite its physical beauty, the couple cautions, "this is a quiet place, not a tourist place." So call this a quiet place with high style: You enter a living area exploding with color and space and feng shui, that ancient Eastern system for creating spatial harmony. Soothing greenery is interspersed among sofas and southwestern-style rugs. Crystals sparkle among the tables, and a striking, azure-blue mosaic tile wall rises from one corner. Guests stay in homey bedrooms decorated with brass beds and flower-covered down comforters. When these rooms are booked, guests for retreat programs may arrange to stay at the Buddhist facility down the way. People from all religious traditions are welcome, and it's not unusual for retreat parties to range from Jesuit priests to Buddhist monks. The usual stay is three days to a week.

The couple offers guests a kind of massage therapy, or Hawaiian bodywork, called "Lomi-lomi," which they say can provoke powerful visions. On the ground floor is a full pharmacy featuring hundreds of herbs and natural medicines, and guests may elect to use some of them for sicknesses or for what's called "a supervised cleansing program." Many guests come for "relationship retreats," where they learn communication and conflict resolution skills and ways to unlock the gifts their relationships hold for them. Lono, a prolific author on spirituality and natural medicine, instructs with his spouse Lani on issues that range from meditation skills to the health implications of drinking water.

Of course, guests may also opt to meditate on their own, a prospect surely enhanced by the surroundings. The retreat center, located on more than two acres, offers wilderness meadows and is adjacent to a protected wilderness area. Guests are welcome to browse and meander along the quiet paths and streams, or settle down on the outdoor deck, which overlooks the vast valley held by Native Americans to be deeply sacred.

Location: Baca Grande subdivision, adjacent to Crestone.

Description: A retreat/holistic center based on ancient Hawaiian spirituality.

Guest Profile: All welcome.

Spiritual Experience: Guests learn about the ancient Hawaiian wisdom of Huna and may choose from a variety of guided or silent retreats. Specialized natural medicine therapies include body cleansing and rebalancing techniques. Spiritual counseling is available for personal and relationship issues, conflict resolution, and mediation.

How to get there: From the white gates as you enter Baca Grande subdivision, go 1.2 miles to Panorama Street (the fifth left past the fire station). Go all the way to the top of Panorama. At the "T" turn right onto Brookview. At the next intersection, which is Pinecone, turn left. Eagle Sanctuary is the second drive on the right.

64. Haidakhandi Universal Ashram

P.O. Box 9
Crestone, CO 81131
719-256-4108
www.babajiashram.org

Ancient Vedic belief and modern ecology join hands in this village-style retreat center tucked into the outer reaches of Crestone's spiritually aware Baca Grande development. "Vedic" refers to the Vedas, the sacred scriptures of ancient India (as opposed to the term "Hindu," which technically refers to the culture). If the thought of conservation linked to religion sounds odd, this ashram will turn you around in no time. As you step onto the 45-acre grounds you'll enter a bee-hive of meditative activity, linked by interesting solar-powered buildings and a lush array of organic farming.

Follow the walkway from the parking area through the grounds and you'll come upon a sight worth a gasp or two: the elegant temple erected to founder and spiritual teacher Haidakhand Babaji. Followers will tell you that although he "left his body" in 1984, this leader, believed to be the descendant of God on Earth, continues to spiritually guide the compound. Devotees may spend hours seated cross-legged, enfolded in the silence of the temple. The centerpiece is an altar/sanctuary dedicated to the Divine Mother, represented by a life-sized marble statue arrayed in a glittering gown and jewels.

As with many Crestone spiritual getaways, a devotee had a vision that Babaji was meant to continue his mission in the Rocky Mountains, says director Ramloti. She began following Babaji in the 1970s and was chosen as national director of U.S. outreach in the mid-1980s. "This is a place where people can come and experience an opening of the heart," she says. Stays range from an hour to a month. But guests should know that while here, they are expected to follow the ashram lifestyle and participate fully in the schedule developed by Babaji himself. The spiritual practices begin at 6 a.m. and include chanting in Sanskrit in the temple. Guests may also join in the daily recitation of the 700 praises of the Divine Mother, which takes just under an hour.

Capacity is roughly 25. Private rooms are available for twice the price of communal rooms, though they still cost less than a good, cheap motel. In addition to following the ashram's spiritual schedule, guests are expected to put in a helping hand for about six hours a day. It's called "Karma Yoga": doing good works for the glory of God's service. "We have no qualms saying, 'Like to help us in the garden? How are you at painting?'" Ramloti says. "It's a blessing to build spiritual centers—it has a tremendous impact on the cosmos."

As they putter and toil around the complex, guests experience ecological living at its most cutting edge. The ashram was built to high environmental specs for the ultimate in sustainable living. The Earthship, as it's called, is one of the ashram's most popular central living spaces. It's made of recycled materials, primarily old tires rammed with earth. Sleeping spaces include a "yurt"—a beehive-shaped design that can sleep up to six—and a straw-bale-and-adobe dormitory with a capacity of 14.

Guests are asked to leave at home all polluting personal-care products like nonbiodegradable shampoos, soaps, and laundry detergents. Here, ecological reverence is part of spirituality: "This is God's home," says Ramloti.

Location: Baca Grande subdivision, adjacent to Crestone.

Description: An ashram that follows the teachings of Haidakhand Babaji, a 20th-century teacher from India, and is dedicated to environmentally sound building practices.

Guest Profile: All welcome. Guests take part in Vedic spiritual exercises and volunteer their help around the ashram.

Spiritual Experience: Immersion in a practical spiritualism in a forested, solitude-rich setting.

How to get there: Take the main Baca Grande road until the pavement ends, and turn right onto Camino Real, which locals call "Two Trees." At the stop sign, take a left onto Wagon Wheel, then another left onto Spanish Creek. You'll start seeing yellow signs for the ashram.

65. Nada Hermitage, Carmelite Spiritual Life Institute

P.O. Box 219 (attn: Sister Connie)
Crestone, CO 81131
719-256-4778
Fax: 719-256-4719
www.spirituallifeinstitute.org

"*A*ll Who Enter Here—No Fuss," tut-tuts the entrance sign, with a twinkle. On that charming but pointed note, guests enter the Nada Hermitage experience, a celebration of "the meeting of man and nature." No fuss, maybe, but you might let loose with a few wows as you first catch sight of this eclectic Spanish-style retreat, rising up from the rugged plains in solitary splendor. It was not by accident that the lines of this graceful adobe haven mimic the symmetry of the nearby 14,000-foot peaks.

Stop your car on the dirt road as you clear the rise. Looking west, it's your first glimpse of the hermitage. If sundown is approaching, the turrets, walkways, and castlelike buttresses will be silhouetted against an eerily beautiful palette of rosy oranges to blue violets, depending on the mood of the waning day. But while your eyes and heart are likely to go on a feasting binge, know that there are strict rules binding guests to the rhythm of solitude. First of all, you are reminded over and over that this is a cloistered monastery. Tourists are invited to pray in the sky-lit chapel during the day, but are begged not to stray into hermitage areas. The strict Thursday-through-Wednesday retreat stay is enforced (unless you make special arrangements) so the monks can help retreatants but keep to their own regular schedule.

Guests stay in adobe hermitages tucked into the wild brush, southwestern style, at ground level and almost invisible from the rugged walkways. Inside, each is a cozy hive with a kitchen and private bath. As for the graceful monastery, one wing is for the hermits: men and women linked by a spiritual community founded in 1960 by the Rev. William McNamara. They follow the spirituality of 16th-century Carmelites St. Teresa of Avila and John of the Cross, and count as their spiritual father the prophet Elijah, the mighty Old Testament figure who, according to scripture and tradition, never died but was spirited up to Heaven in a fiery chariot.

As action-packed as that scriptural scene is, it's solitude and reflection that Nada stresses at this 8,000-foot getaway. When you arrive, a monk takes on a temporary role as spiritual director to help you get oriented. But you are expected to exert enough inner resources to enter into the wilderness experience on your own. Let "the Spirit within be your director," urges the brochure. Guests are invited to join in on Saturday chores.

The hermitage is ecumenical and available to people of all faiths or none. Day guests are welcome to stroll the main pathways and pray in the chapel, a serene space lit by skylight—perfect for meditative reading—and flanked by stained glass. A tabernacle is located directly behind an altar of rough-hewn stone. The crucifix is an unusual depiction of a suffering Jesus Christ, eyes open wide and staring intently into the distance.

The intense, enforced solitude apparently makes this hermitage unforgettable to its retreatants. "Here, no fakery is possible," writes one. "Here you face yourself, the earth, and God naked. Nada."

Location: Baca Grande subdivision, adjacent to Crestone.

Description: A retreat and contemplation center run by a small monastic community of hermits, both men and women, which is characterized by "earthy mysticism and a Christian humanism."

Guest Profile: All welcome. The monastery asks you to arrange your retreat to begin on a Thursday afternoon, with departure the following Wednesday before noon.

Spiritual Experience: A vast area of mountain and plains offering plenty of space for intense solitude. Minimal direction from a monk available.

How to get there: Enter the subdivision on the main road, Camino Baca Grande. Drive about 1.5 miles, looking to the right for a street named Rendezvous Way. (All street signs are low, near the ground.) Take Rendezvous west, toward the mountains. Drive the equivalent of a few blocks to the monastery.

66. Sacred Passage and the Way of Nature

877-818-1881
E-mail: info@sacredpassage.com
www.sacredpassage.com

*W*alk into John Milton's world, leave it forever changed.

Environmentalist, adventurer, spiritual teacher, Milton is a unique guide to those seeking to turn a sharp corner in their spiritual life. Milton offers the most ancient and intense of "organized" spiritual retreats: vision quest. The intense, four-day experience is endured, naked, within an 8-foot circle bereft of food, water, and sleep. In Native American cultures people took up vision quests during important "threshold" times in their lives, says Milton. They come out of them drained of ordinary, limiting reality, having "looked into the eye of the Cosmos…and having experienced everything as part of oneself."

Milton promises much the same today. Those who commit to a vision quest under his guidance should expect to encounter "an inner vision and experience deeper realities." Milton says he's trained all sorts of folks—even 80-year-olds—for the intense and challenging personal adventure. But the process takes about a year of training, which, obviously, must be meticulously arranged ahead of time. For details go to Milton's website.

For spiritual seekers with either less time or more caution, there is Sacred Passage, Milton's less intense retreat program, which he describes as a "wilderness solo." You must reserve 12 days for the total experience, including 5 days of training. The seeker goes into the wilderness alone with a tent, clothing, and water, remaining close enough to signal for help (a loud whistle is included in the equipment) and just 15 minutes from Milton's cabin, located at the edge of Crestone and national forest land. In those six days and nights, seekers experience a transforming relationship with "formless spirit and nature and feel themselves one with the body of Mother Earth," says Milton. He prepares seekers with Buddhist and Taoist meditations and ancient shamanic practices, many of which regard Earth as a sacred temple.

But Milton is more than a cosmic spiritual director. An explorer and author, he is a founder of a worldwide environmental movement. If supporters of Earth Day and Greenpeace could point to a genesis moment—their own "shot heard round the world"—a good candidate would be the 1965 publication of Milton's book, *The Future Environments of North America.* Milton acquired his backcountry survival skills the hard way—he earned them. He led an expedition into the last uncharted portions of the Rocky Mountains in the Logan Range in Canada, and his account of getting his team out alive from the blizzard-gripped Brooks Range resulted in the 1970 book, *Nameless Valleys, Shining Mountains.* The grandson of a New Jersey senator and Mayflower pilgrims (with a nip of Native American blood), Milton says he did his own first vision quest at age seven with his parents' blessing. He came upon the idea, he says, not from history books but from an inner primordial knowledge that is part of the human race.

Today, Milton is part of the worldwide ecological movement that would reconfigure governments and legal systems to put Earth first—"to see Earth and all of life as your personal family." In Crestone, he founded the Sacred Land Trust, which is working initially on purchasing and preserving 360 acres of Crestone land as a vast and sacred "Church of the Earth." Its mission is only an acknowledgment of what was there before: the most sacred of all lands.

Location: The heart of Crestone.

Description: "An experiential and powerful retreat experience" designed to provide spiritual solutions and help the participant attain higher states of consciousness.

Guest Profile: Anyone who passes muster.

Spiritual Experience: Intense and rigorous.

How to get there: Call and arrange for John Milton to meet you.

67. Sanctuary House

P.O. Box 332
Crestone, CO 81131
719-256-4420
Fax: 719-256-4420
www.sanctuaryhouse.org

*O*riginally inspired by a popular Christian meditative technique known as centering prayer, William and Barbara Howell broadened that focus to embrace an array of world religions. To celebrate their expanded view, the couple relocated to Crestone and opened Sanctuary House. It's a tribute—and an imaginative one at that—to what Barbara calls "the mystical side of all traditions."

In the handsome, circular compound, the Howells have included four chapels dedicated to four major wisdom traditions: Judeo/Christian, Tibetan Buddhist, Hindu/Vedic, and Sufi/Muslim. When completed, the center courtyard of the large, circular complex will contain a labyrinth, an exact replica of the 800-year-old original that graces the floor of Chartres Cathedral in France. The chapels are small enclosures, most comfortable for two to four at a time.

In a creative touch, when guests enter they are immediately suffused with the fragrance of that particular tradition. In other words, Christians contemplating the crucifix on their small benches are surrounded by Western-style incense. Those seated cross-legged before replicas of the Hindu Trinity are enveloped by the sharp spices of India. An Oriental, Tibetan scent enfolds guests seated before the Buddhist prayer flags. And in the Sufi mosque, the fragrance of Arabian spices drifts by pillars and Persian rugs.

Guests stay in private retreat apartments, which

Location: Chalet of Baca Grande subdivision, adjacent to Crestone.

Description: A multireligious retreat center "in the round."

Guest Profile: All are welcome.

Spiritual Experience: Guests may participate in spiritual practices and events at Sanctuary House or concentrate on a silent retreat experience.

How to get there: Take the main road in the Baca Grande subdivision until the pavement ends. Turn right onto Camino Real ("Two Trees" to locals). Go to the first stop sign, and turn left on Wagonwheel. Go 2 miles to the end of the pavement and turn left. Follow the small, white, arrow-shaped signs, bordered in blue, that say "Sanctuary House."

include winding staircases reminiscent of medieval castles. These aeries, which give the impression of being above the treetops, are furnished with private baths and kitchens. Balconies overlook the labyrinth in the courtyard.

Retreatants also have access to various organized meditative sessions conducted by the Howells. The repertoire of spiritual exercises includes Zikr, a remembrance of the Divine in the Muslim tradition, which William has studied to an expert level. He leads guests, assembled in a circle, as they chant the praises of Allah. The Howells are followers of Swami Punit Acharyaji (affectionately known as "Bapu"), an Indian Yogi mystic who teaches a mantra that adherents of any religion can use to reach a deeper connection to the Divine.

The Howells still embrace Christian mysticism and centering prayer. They were part of the original group that learned centering prayer from the Rev. Thomas Keating, a Trappist monk who lives at St. Benedict's Monastery near Snowmass (see page 221). Keating is credited with developing the centering prayer methodology, which Barbara says may best be described as a method of prayer that accesses the Divine within. Now they pass what they have found inside themselves along to others. Guests, however, may decide the level of their involvement in the organized spirituality offered at Sanctuary House. Above all else, says Howell, "we want to offer beauty and sacred space."

68. Sri Aurobindo Learning Center

P.O. Box 88
Crestone, CO 81131
719-256-4822 or 719-256-4917
Fax: 719-256-4908
E-mail: rodhemsell@yahoo.com
www.auroville.org
www.miraura.org

Location: Center of the Baca Grande development adjacent to Crestone.

Description: A spiritual center that fosters the teachings of Hindu philosopher Sri Aurobindo.

Guest Profile: Scholars and those interested in learning more about the philosopher's life work. Some long-time disciples live on the grounds.

Spiritual Experience: Meditation and study form the annual weeklong seminar, held in the summer (times and dates vary). Other times of the year, guests may stop to pick up literature and information.

How to get there: From Crestone, go into the Baca Grande development and turn left at the first street sign onto Baca Grant Way. (If you pass the fire station, you've gone too far.) Continue three blocks and look for a sign on the right marked "Savitri House."

Philosopher, poet, and Hindu yogi Sri Aurobindo, Indian-born and Cambridge-educated, is well known among followers of both Eastern and Western thought. During his life, from 1872 to 1950, Aurobindo's ashram in southern India, called Pondicherry, became a sought-after place of learning. It in turn led to Auroville, a namesake town that grew up around it. Known as the City of Human Unity, Auroville is the center for Aurobindo's lifelong pursuit of what he called "Integral Yoga," or the spiritual transformation of mind, life, and body.

"He envisioned an evolution in spiritual consciousness," explains Rod Hemsell, president of the Sri Aurobindo Learning Center Foundation in Crestone. Writers from Aldous Huxley to Alan Watts have admired the philosopher's work. But followers and scholars needn't go to India to immerse themselves in his distinctive practice of "devotion, study, and work." Crestone is one of several Western sites with an Aurobindo center.

Rod Hemsell, president of the Sri Aurobindo Learning Center Foundation, at the Savitri House Meditation dome. Photo courtesy of Rod Hemsell.

Guests may pause here to learn more, as the complex includes a library and a meditation dome. For those with a background and serious interest in Aurobindo's philosophy, there is a weeklong workshop every summer. Overnight accommodations are available in nearby townhouses and an inn while guests take part in the meditation and study program.

Aurobindo amassed the résumés of several men. He was by turns a newspaperman, a politician, a pre-Gandhi advocate of nonviolent resistance, and a prisoner—spending a year in a British prison for agitating for Indian independence. But his most lasting fame has come from his volumes of prose and poetry, which earned him, Hemsell says, a nomination for the Nobel Prize in literature. Aurobindo's greatest prose work, *The Life Divine*, synthesized yoga practice, psychology, and Eastern and Western philosophy in more than 1,000 pages. His greatest poem, *Savitri* (the name of the goddess of illumined speech), took 20 years to write and is one of the longest narrative poems in the English language. As read by Aurobindo scholars and disciples, the poem is a mantra that followers use to achieve spiritual illumination.

No mention of Aurobindo's life would be complete without paying tribute to his spiritual co-worker, known to disciples as The Mother. Hemsell explains that she is regarded as the female incarnation, or channel, of the divine feminine. Prior to her death in 1973 she established Auroville to ensure that Sri Aurobindo's work would endure. Soon, westerners were seeking out Auroville and spreading the message. Two of them were Hanne and Maurice Strong of Crestone. In 1986, the Strongs invited Seyril Schochen, a disciple of Sri Aurobindo, to open one of the first spiritual centers in the Crestone development of the Baca Grande.

Today, a host of other spiritual philosophies have joined the Sri Aurobindo Learning Center in Crestone. But in a way unforeseen, perhaps, by Aurobindo himself, his presence here has helped achieve one of his lifelong goals: to transform society into a shared human experience of spiritual consciousness. For it's here, in the Baca Grande, that the Strongs have created what they believe is "the largest intentional interfaith ecumenical community in North America."

69. Karma Thegsum Tashi Gomang

The Tibetan Project House
P.O. Box 39 (159 Moonlight Way)
Crestone, CO 81131
719-256-4695

$\mathcal{W}$elcome to a vigorous and lively center for the study and practice of Buddhism. While the following may not mean much to neophytes, experienced Buddhist practitioners may find it helpful to know that Karma Thegsum is affiliated with Karma Triyana Dharmachakra in Woodstock, New York, and is under the auspices of Gyalwa Karmapa, supreme head of the Kagyu Order of Tibetan Buddhism.

This involved and energized retreat and teaching center has much going on. Its plans are to build a monastery and the first Tibetan medical center in the western hemisphere. Two retreat cabins are complete: one minimalist, with hand-pumped kitchen sink and outhouse, the other with full indoor plumbing and kitchen facilities. The daily one-hour meditation

Location: Baca Grande subdivision, adjacent to Crestone.

Description: A multidimensional Buddhist center for teaching and spirituality.

Guest Profile: Those interested in exploring Buddhist practices.

Spiritual Experience: As individual as the individual.

How to get there: Enter the Baca Grande subdivision on Camino Baca Grande. Drive to Moonlight Way (the first left turn after the firehouse, which is also on the left), near the subdivision entrance. Take Moonlight to the first house on the left. You'll recognize it by the colorful Buddhist prayer flags.

schedule starts at 7 a.m. and Sunday evenings at 7 p.m. Educational opportunities include teaching seminars by Tibetan masters including physicians of Tibetan medicine.

The center has also built a great stupa—a shrine that repre-sents, in concrete form, the enlightened mind of the Buddha. The Tashi Gomang stupa took seven years to complete and was consecrated in 1996. Another one— Enlightenment Stupa, known locally as "Little Stupa"— was built on land originally owned by James George, the Canadian ambassador to India in the 1950s. When China invaded Tibet, George helped build in India an exile settlement for the Tibetan people. Consecrated in 1984, Little Stupa is dedicated to Padmasambhava, founder of Tibetan Buddhism.

To get to the Tashi Gomang stupa: Take Camino Baca Grande to the end of the pavement. There it meets Camino Real, a nicely paved road leading south that locals call "Two Trees." Continue to the stop sign, which is at Wagon Wheel, another paved road. Turn left and drive to the end of the pavement. Go left again, toward the mountains. When you can go no farther, turn right and be on the lookout for a "Stupa" sign. Look for a rugged, unfinished parking area. You now have a one-mile hike to the stupa. (If the gate is open, you can try driving to the stupa on the narrow dirt road, but locals say it's nearly impossible to negotiate should you meet a vehicle coming the other way.)

To get to Little Stupa: Follow the directions above to Wagon Wheel. Instead of staying on that road to the top, take the very first right. Keep going straight until you see the stupa.

The great Tashi Gomang stupa at Karma Thegsum Tashi Gomang, Crestone, was consecrated in 1996.

Sacred Places

70. Blanca Peak

This is a region not just to visit, but in which to be steeped in the sacred history of the land. Since ancient times, Blanca Peak, rising 14,345 feet in the majestic Sangre de Cristo Range, has held a special place in Native American history. Known by the Navajo as Sisnaajini, "Strength of White Gem Beads," it is the tallest and most authoritative of four mountains that form the boundaries of what ancient Indian lore calls "the greatest sanctuary," a massive triangle arching over three states.

With a map and a pen, you can bring this ancient holy area to life in front of your eyes. (It's worth remembering that ancient peoples had neither modern maps nor satellite views when they created this perfect geometric landscape stretching over thousands of square miles.) First, peg Blanca as the easternmost pillar. Then draw a straight line southwest to Durango and locate the second pillar, Mt. Hesperus. Continue southwest to Flagstaff, Arizona, and find Abalone Mountain. Then point your pen toward Albuquerque and locate Mt. Taylor, directly west of the city.

You are looking at a perfect triangle, with Blanca as the crown jewel. Navajo teachings consider Hesperus the ruling place over the underworld, Taylor the pillar of government, and Abalone the site of the New Dawn and arbiter between Earth and the universe. Blanca is at the heart of Mother Earth, anchored to the planet with a thunderbolt and the site where humanity began, according to many Native American histories.

Get to Blanca Peak off of Highway 150, 14 miles south of Great Sand Dunes National Park (see page 192). For more information, call 719-378-2312.

71. Culturally Peeled Trees

Photo courtesy of Marilyn Martorano

*A*n unusual ancient phenomenon in this region is the "culturally peeled trees," a familiar sight in the Great Sand Dunes National Park and Wilderness Area. You may check out an example at the park's visitors' center. "We started seeing all these ponderosa pine trees with huge scars on them," recalls archaeologist Marilyn Martorano, who went on to write her master's thesis about the unusual findings. She found that Native Americans sought out these towering, 300- to 400-year-old trees as a kind of mini grocery store. In their bark was wholesome food, which could be used for emergency sustenance, natural carbo-loading, or a sweet treat. Scientific testing shows it to be calcium-rich—one pound of inner bark has the calcium of nine glasses of milk—and is also believed to be high in vitamin C, zinc, and iron.

Following the guidance of Native Americans, Martorano learned how to peel the trees herself, using tools available to ancient peoples. Done correctly, the peeling doesn't harm the tree—an early form of environment-friendly recycling. She found the inner meat "slightly sweet tasting and very fibrous, spongy, and moist." Among its other many amazing properties, the versatile substance is believed to have been ground into a flour and fashioned into a poultice for wounds, or even a kind of adhesive or waterproofing material.

Are there spiritual properties as well? Nobody's talking. Archaeologists such as Martorano say Native Americans have asked that certain parts of their ancient lore be protected from public scrutiny. (If you wonder at the sensitivity, consider that Blanca Peak's reputation has drawn flocks of UFO enthusiasts, some of whom claim to have witnessed spaceship landings and mysterious strobe-and-light shows playing on her flanks.) Even the more humble peeled-trees phenomenon is vulnerable to misuse: "The Utes have told us some things but the information is not considered public knowledge," Martorano says. "We're trying to earn their trust so we can help the park manage the trees. We're trying to learn more to help us see the spiritual side."

The park entrance is northeast of Alamosa. From Alamosa, go east 16 miles on Highway 160. Turn left on Highway 150 and go 16 miles north to the entrance of the park. For more information, call the park at 719-378-2312.

72. Great Sand Dunes National Park

Colorado's portion of the sacred triangle, anchored by Blanca Peak (see page 189), includes a mind-bending landscape of 700-foot-high sand dunes and other features highly prized as sacred and/or significant in Native American cultures. To this day, visitors should have no problem understanding why this hauntingly beautiful landscape, now memorialized as Great Sand Dunes National Park and Wilderness Area, has been considered a treasure both in ancient times and now—or why Crestone has evolved into an international gathering place for the world's religions.

For centuries, the vast plains that spill westward from the Sand Dunes and the Sangre de Cristos have been highly revered, too. From any deck or porch in the Baca Grande subdivision, you are gazing west across a noble landscape. This was the gathering place for many tribes, who called this the Bloodless Valley, a place where all weapons would be laid aside and peace would reign. Modern guests may still contemplate some of the ways Native Americans sealed this land as special—as a place to commune in peace and to meditate on sacred things. To grasp the many ancient spiritual meanings here, Great Sand Dunes National Park and Wilderness Area is a great place to start.

The park entrance is northeast of Alamosa. From Alamosa, go east 16 miles on Highway 160. Turn left on Highway 150 and go 16 miles north to the entrance of the park. For more information, call the park at 719-378-2312 or go to www.alamosa.org.

73. Meditation Seats

The San Luis Valley contains other ancient artifacts with more defined spiritual meanings. For example, meditation seats dot the landscape, according to John Milton, a spiritual teacher, guide, and preservationist.

"We're talking about something that's off the charts spiritually," Milton says. He discovered the natural stone seats 20 or 30 years ago but kept his find quiet to discourage curiosity seekers. The seats are stone formations probably used by ancient shamans, or spiritual

Author and environmentalist John Milton in the field at one of the meditation seats thought to have been used by ancient shamans.

teachers, that "allow one to sit comfortably and make a special connection with nature and spirit." Milton, whose multidimensional résumé includes a lifetime spent as an explorer and early spokesman for the worldwide environmental movement, has created the Sacred Land Trust to preserve ancient Native American sites for posterity. "This area has a density and frequency of sacred sites that is probably ten times greater than any other natural area in Colorado or the Southwest," Milton says. Hook up with Milton and his Sacred Passage program (see Sacred Passage and the Way of Nature, page 180) and you can see the ancient meditation seats.

Other Spiritual Destinations

For directions or other information about the destinations below, contact the parties directly or call the Manitou Foundation (719-256-4267) or the Manitou Institute (719-256-4265). You can also try the Crestone Business Association at 719-256-4110 or www.crestone.org. You might want to talk with Ken and Lynda Kucin, owners of the Desert Sage Restaurant (719-256-4402). Lynda is the editor of *Crestone: An Illustrated Guide to the Significant Attractions of the Crestone/Baca Area,* which contributed some of the information below. The maps in her guide would be very helpful for getting around the quirky Crestone area. The Desert Sage was built to serve the movers and shakers of the Aspen Institute, which later relocated from this area (see Introduction, page 158). Today, whether you're a mover, a shaker, or just here for quiet retreat, it's still a good and convenient place to dine, located right at the gate to the Baca Grande subdivision.

Manitou Foundation Solitary Retreat Hermitage Project
A proposal to create opportunities for experienced and dedicated religious practitioners to live in mountain solitude for extended periods. The project's first goal is to complete three single-room retreat cabins in the Sangre de Cristo wilderness.

Ziggurat
Located at the far south end of the Baca Grande subdivision. This copy of an ancient Assyrian prayer tower was built by Najeeb Halaby, a prominent Arab American whose daughter, Lisa, became Queen Noor when she married King Hussein of Jordan.

Like many Crestone-area destinations, this site is rather difficult to find—the better to appreciate when you arrive. Enter the Baca Grande subdivision on Camino Baca Grande, and take that road to the end of the pavement. There it meets Camino Real, a paved road leading south. Continue to the stop sign, which is at Wagon Wheel, another paved road. Take Wagon Wheel, which will curve and eventually meet Cottonwood Creek Road. Look for the intersection with Staghorn Road. Go left, and the Ziggurat should soon become visible.

The Crestone Mountain Zen Center welcomes serious students and practitioners of Buddhist meditation for year-round training.

Region Six:
Western Slope South

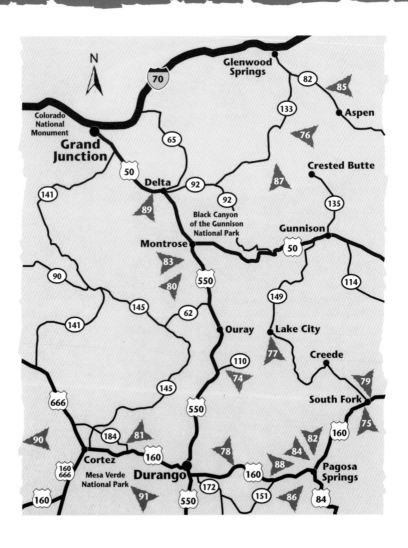

*N*o other place in the United States can offer this: a steady line of spiritual stops all nestled against the western spine of the Continental Divide. An adventurer in the sacred could pile into a car and take in a dozen retreat places just by meandering southward down the state. Another handful are a little farther west, near Grand Junction and Durango. The journey along the Divide takes in some of the most majestic sights in the world. Perhaps this is God's choice for God's country.

It's no small thing to be standing next to a miner's shrine several hundred feet above the town of Silverton, jagged peaks bearing down on three sides with only the murmur of the wind to accompany your prayer. This is the region for about a dozen evangelical Christian retreat camps tucked away in picturesque backcountry forests and mountain aeries, too. They specialize in welcoming kids in the summer and adults and church groups the rest of the year. Other Christian sanctuaries range from a prominent Benedictine monastery to a family-run center set in a geodesic dome overlooking a meadow.

You can also find an internationally recognized retreat center in the Tibetan Buddhist tradition, and a charming and serene holistic center that gives every sign of delivering what's promised in its name: Spirit Rest.

Sanctuaries

74. Christ of the Mines Shrine

$\mathcal{O}$nce your heart stops galloping from the thrill of driving Red Mountain Pass—and from taking in the thin air at 9,000-plus feet—you're in for another kind of uplifting moment in the mountain aerie of Silverton.

On a grassy rise high above this lovely old mining village stands a towering statue of Jesus Christ, arms outstretched and beckoning. A large stone ledge furnishes a quiet place to sit and contemplate the statue's majestic face. Or, you can swing around and face the speech-defying grandeur of the scene before you: a tiny village far below, cuddled in the embrace of sharp peaks. You may well catch sight of the Durango/Silverton tourist train as it pulls into town.

The shrine is backed by a grove of trees. So cozy and contemplative is this place that if you happen to be alone or with comfortable company, you may well be inspired to pray aloud or even sing a hymn. A plaque at the base of the statue explains the origins of this noble spot: "This shrine," it begins, "erected in honor of Christ of the Mines by the people of Silverton to ask God's blessing on the mining industry of the San Juans, 1958–1959. In thanksgiving to Christ of the Mines for deliverance of the entire workforce when Lake Emma flooded, Sunnyside Mine, June 4."

As testament to this place's power to inspire, visitors have turned a brochure stand into an impromptu altar of praise and prayer. Lift the drawer and inside you'll find notes, cards, even small stuffed animals asking for prayers or expressing thanks to God for favors received. One note, scrawled on the back of a torn bottled-water label, begins: "Thank you, Lord, for my wonderful family! Thank you for bringing us here!"

Location: A hillside that overlooks the town of Silverton. Once you know the shrine is there, you can see it from anywhere in town or from nearby roadways.

Description: A sacred place for reflection.

Guest Profile: All welcome.

Spiritual Experience: Solitude and peace, intensified by your perch high above the bustling activity of a small town, with mountain vistas stretching before you.

How to get there: On Highway 110 at Silverton, if you're coming from the north, watch carefully for a little Forest Service sign pointing left to "Miners Shrine." It's at the southern end of Red Mountain Pass just outside town. From the other direction, the sign appears just as you're leaving town, at the beginning of your ascent up 110. Drive half a mile up the dirt road to a small parking area. From there, it's a fairly bracing 100 paces more up a slope to the statue.

Retreats

75. Beaver Creek Youth Camp

P.O. Box 186
South Fork, CO 84154
719-873-5311
or 719-852-2141 (attn: Art Sullivan)

*I*n the rough-hewn beauty of a glacier's ancient resting place, this Methodist youth camp has been drawing summer campers since shortly after World War II. Huge boulders and towering stands of ponderosa pine and Douglas fir create a cozy retreat area for the sturdy cabins and lodge.

The month of July is reserved for young Methodists. There are separate cabin clusters for boys and girls. Other times of the year this rustic camp is leased to family reunions, church groups, and socially significant nonprofits such as Alcoholics Anonymous. Guests pray and attend services at a lovely outdoor "chapel" called the Green Cathedral, a rustic hideaway marked by a pulpit surrounded by trees and boulders. To protect its nonprofit church mission—and to follow the desires of its founders—every group is asked to hold regular prayer times and sing grace before meals.

Location: Boulder-strewn forestland about 6 miles outside of South Fork.

Description: A rugged camp for youth and groups.

Guest Profile: Nonprofit and family groups welcome; United Methodist youth use the camp during summer.

Spiritual Experience: As solitary as one wishes in the deep forest. Groups using the grounds are expected to build a spiritual component and prayer time into their programs.

How to get there: At the western edge of South Fork on Highway 160, look for a sign marked "Forest Service access road." You can only turn south. The newly paved road takes you 3.1 miles to the turnoff, which is just after you pass a sign for Million Reservoir. Signs will clearly lead you to the campsite.

The camp is bounded by a deep river gorge, 40 feet down, called Bear Creek. The rough and tumbling creek becomes the punch line for a joke during the first night's orientation session: "You're not to take a step off the property unless you take a counselor with you." After they get their laugh, the staff makes sure new guests and nighttime strollers know that they're serious about safety in this backcountry haven. One cabin even tells the tale: It's marked by the gouged bite of a visiting bear.

76. Camp Id-Ra-Ha-Je West

27862 County Road 12
Somerset, CO 81434
970-929-5221
Fax: 970-929-5200
www.campwest.com

*N*ear the banks of the Anthracite River lies a church camp whose name defines its mission: "I'd Rather Have Jesus." The first letters of each word of that old hymn title form the name for a series of Christian camps founded by a Texas pastor dating back to the 1940s. Colorado has another Camp Id-Ra-Ha-Je, outside Bailey (see page 112).

As you wind down the dirt road, then clatter over an unusual metal bridge spanning the Anthracite, you'll come upon a classic camp scene, in which a pretty campus "green" is surrounded by cabins

Location: A two-hour drive from Grand Junction, the camp's main supply station.

Description: Interactive, high-activity camp.

Guest Profile: Kids and groups.

Spiritual Experience: Interactive programs, with solitude getaways available in the surrounding Raggeds Wilderness.

How to get there: From Glenwood Springs/Carbondale, take Highway 82 to Highway 133. Go south to the end of Paonia Reservoir. Look for signs for Kebler Pass, Gunnison, and Crested Butte. (From the Grand Junction/Delta direction, the signs are at your arrival to the reservoir.) Turn down a sharp, winding road that takes you past a pretty restaurant/gift shop area. Follow the dirt road another 3 miles, and watch closely for a small camp sign on the right.

cupped in the embrace of granite cliffs. Scalloped eaves give these rustic buildings a homespun air. Encircling the scene are the granite cliffs of the Raggeds Wilderness.

First priority is running a summer camp for kids that emphasizes a close personal relationship with Jesus Christ. The next priority is offering retreat time to neighboring churches and religious groups who help with camp upkeep and support. Here, the word "neighbor" is a matter of heart, not geography: Some longtime supporters come from as far away as Michigan to help with periodic painting and cleanup work.

As Labor Day nears, the camp hosts Christian-centered events for adults and kids, such as Family Camp, which brings in nationally known spiritual motivators and musical groups for retreats spanning several days. In the remaining months—excluding the closed months of November and December—the camp is available to nonprofits with a mission of social service.

Accommodations are rustic. A typical cabin holds five double bunks, eighty in all. The camp spreads people out more in the winter, since only some cabins are heated (by propane), and many adults don't cotton to climbing onto top bunks. A central lodge area is furnished with a new woodstove, as well as serviceable old recliners and sofas plus TV, Ping-Pong, and foosball tables.

77. Camp Redcloud

P.O. Box 130
Lake City, CO 81235
970-944-2625
Fax: 970-944-2602
www.campredcloud.org

*N*ot for nothing does this camp call itself "A Christian Challenge Center." In these towering San Juans, young Christians test themselves and come closer to God as they ride horses, rappel down cliffs, traverse rivers, climb craggy peaks, and plunge down trails on their mountain bikes. Safety is the number-one goal on all activities. Each outing is overseen by a large staff of young, vigorous Christians as eager to plunge into the Gospel message of Jesus Christ as they are the nearby Rio Grande. The staff likes to say that this is not a "pamper camp" and that kids will be challenged physically and spiritually.

Location: 9,200 feet up, 9 miles southwest of Lake City.

Description: A high-activity Christian camp.

Guest Profile: Youth, adults, and special groups.

Spiritual Experience: Solitude getaways abound.

How to get there: Heading south from Lake City on Highway 149, watch very carefully for the County Road 30 sign. Turn right (west). You'll pass Lake San Cristobal. Stay on the paved road about 4 miles. When you come to a dirt road, stay right (don't go over the bridge), and drive 3 miles. The camp, on your left, is a stunner as you come upon it across a wide meadow. If you're coming from the south, drive over Slumgullion Pass on Highway 149 and proceed toward Lake City. A sign for the Alfred Packer massacre site means you're getting close to Highway 30. Look closely for the turn, which is a hard left.

The setting of this camp, named after the nearby Fourteener, Redcloud Peak, is glorious. The complex itself is tucked into a wide meadowland flanked by tiers of peaks and lovely, fjordlike valleys. The heart of the camp, a close-knit series of buildings, resembles a bustling gold rush town. The well-landscaped, stone-lined paths meander to a series of new resort-quality cabins. Unlike more rustic camps, these are equipped with electricity and sinks. What's more, thoughtful architecture gives bunkmates breathing room: They are spaced out in groups of two, not squashed together row after row.

Run by an interdenominational nonprofit group (the board of directors hails from Colorado, Texas, and Chicago), the camp brings its own volunteer building crews, who are expanding the complex into huge new staff buildings and overnight accommodations. Besides a summer camp for youth, it's available for family and group retreats and many special events, such as sports camps featuring National Hockey League players.

The crown jewel is the chapel, also built by volunteers and sitting at the pinnacle of a grassy hill. The chapel's huge windows, which fill the back sanctuary wall, open onto a soaring, fir-studded, snowcapped mountainside.

78. Cross Bar X Youth Ranch

2111 County Road 222
Durango, CO 81303
970-259-2716
Fax: 970-259-8006
www.crossbarxcamp.org

*T*his youth camp makes a good first impression—especially when you've just surprised the young, coed teen staff celebrating their last night together with a quiet candlelight steak dinner.

They were celebrating a summer's work well done. The camp's clientele, mostly disadvantaged and urban kids who stay for one- or two-week stints, have left behind a wide mesa that offers a stunning, near-360-degree view of the La Plata Range. The major requirement of the young, polite staff is that they be sure-footed Christians, able to communicate the message "that Jesus Christ is the one and only Son of God who died for our sins." That message is wrapped in a sunup-to-sundown array of robust activities. There are mountain bike and obstacle courses, BB and archery ranges, a swimming hole (lifeguards on duty), and even a small farm of chickens, goats, lambs, and ducks. Horses are available for riding.

Location: About 12 miles southeast of Durango.

Description: "A special Bible-centered camp to help low-income and inner-city youth overcome today's challenges."

Guest Profile: Youth, 8 to 18 years old.

Spiritual Experience: Activity-oriented in a rugged outdoor setting.

How to get there: Take Highway 160 east out of Durango. Watch for a right turn onto County Road 222. It's very obscured, so mark your crumbs this way: When you reach the intersection in Durango where Highway 550 peels off to Farmington, New Mexico, you are 4.7 miles away from your turn. Go east on 160 and look very closely for the yellow, cross-shaped highway sign marking 222.

Parents may be relieved to know that boys and girls use the camp on separate weeks, and that they are overseen by staff of the same gender. (During that week, the opposite-gendered staff works on administrative duties and cleanup.) Four cabins, minus electricity, are available for the kids—who love the idea of bumping around with flashlights, anyway. The main lodge, with separate accommodations for the coed staff and dining facilities, is a sturdy and attractive log cabin with a wide porch for drinking in the scenery. In non-summer months, adults and nonprofit groups such as AA or the Christian Motorcycle Association get dibs on the camp, and can stay in the more comfy lodge.

79. Living Rock Christian Retreat

0278 Shirley Drive
South Fork, CO 81154
719-873-5215

*T*his breathtaking, cliff-edge site was once home to a racy nightclub and gambling den. Its destiny was to pass into the hands of an intensely evangelical, Bible-honing Christian couple who would have considered it sinful to have ever darkened its door.

On that interesting, contradictory note, O. V. Keith and his wife, Tommy, have fashioned a retreat getaway for adults, church groups, singles, and couples. While the center is interdenominational, the Keiths

Location: The eastern edge of South Fork.

Description: A ranch-home retreat center for Bible-believing Christians and those seeking to become Christians.

Guest Profile: Groups and adults comfortable with a Bible-based Christian retreat program.

Spiritual Experience: Guests take part in a retreat program, either their own or one fashioned by the retreat owners.

How to get there: From the center of South Fork head east on Highway 160. Look for Highway 19, the equivalent of a few city blocks from the center of town. Turn left (north). In a heartbeat you'll cross a small bridge over the Rio Grande River and be at the end of the very short road, which veers both right and left. Go right, and wind your way up a few hundred yards to the house.

expect guests to be comfortable with their deeply held, born-again beliefs. The Keiths hail from the born-again revival circuit and are founders of Spiritual Fitness Ministries. Today, they concentrate on sharing the message of Jesus Christ from the 7,000-square-foot ranch home with a "past." It can accommodate up to 60 guests, who stay in dorm-style rooms. A limited number of private rooms are also available. The minimum stay is three days, and guests must either provide their own spiritual program or accept the one provided by the hosts.

While the house itself is still a work in progress—the men's dorm still rests on the scraped-up floor where the bar once stood—the eight-acre setting is inspiring indeed. The lodge's pride and joy, the "great room" living area, is furnished in a homey style and serves as the dining area where home-cooked meals are served. Its gasp-factor comes from the banks of windows facing north and south: Each opens up onto the kind of vista that could launch a travelogue. Guests behold the outskirts of South Fork, a sheer drop below. The Rio Grande stretches into the distance. From here, the Keiths say they can count eight of Colorado's mighty Fourteeners and gaze for a hundred miles into the Sangre de Cristos and the famous Great Sand Dunes area.

80. Mountaintop Retreat

63451 Ida Road
Montrose, CO 81401
970-240-4431
Fax: 800-411-6976
E-mail: camp@mountaintopretreat.com
www.mountaintopretreat.com

*T*he mission here is to evangelize the lost—and they don't mean those making their way from Montrose. Your reward at the end of the journey is 35 acres of meditative beauty overlooking the vast Uncompahgre Valley. Sitting high on a mesa, the center is a network of lovely, intimate arborways of well-pruned scrub pine, mahogany, and piñon pines. Though not intentional, the effect may remind you of Japanese-style ikebana artistry, with the closely cropped branches zigzagging their way to the sky and creating dappled fingers of light along the many footpaths.

But above all, this is a hardy, rustic camp for interacting and having fun—and spreading the good news of Jesus Christ. Its entrance sign spells out the goal: "Come Stay a While, Play a While, Be Still a While."

First priority is the summer camp for kids, some of whom are from families that have come here for three generations. A specialty is helping those who are struggling with their faith. Mornings are spent in Bible classes and prayer, afternoons in the myriad activities on the sprawling acreage. They live in no-nonsense, hard-sided A-frames with canvas for doors and windows.

All day long, kids are encouraged to be reflective and examine their lives in light of the Gospel. At nightfall they move to a large campfire area marked with wooden benches, where they share their Christian testimony, wrestle with their problems, and pray. Camp leaders say wonderful conversions of spirit happen at the campfire, as kids unburden themselves under legions of stars while the pines whisper and canyons echo with the eerie howls of coyotes.

Daylight offers many well-planned activities. One favorite is the "zip-line," which plummets the harnessed-in rider along a 370-foot line, 18 feet high, suspended between two poles—and offers a bird's-eye view of the valley and entire range. There's a 250-foot water slide as well as volleyball and basketball.

In the non-summer months, adults have all that available, too—plus countless meditative footpaths. Theoretically, it's possible to follow these paths from camp through a national forest all the way to Grand Junction, 100 miles away. Even within the camp, many areas are wild backcountry, and guests are not allowed beyond a certain point unless accompanied by guide-certified camp leaders. During adult season, living arrangements become more substantial and move onto one floor of the attractive main lodge. That building also includes a cheerfully sunny dining room overlooking the Gunnison National Forest and a blue-tinged mountain range.

Location: About 15 miles outside Montrose.

Description: A rugged, high-activity camp dedicated to sharing the Gospel and strengthening families.

Guest Profile: Youth, families, couples, and adults.

Spiritual Experience: Geared to guests involved in interactive spiritual programs, with solitude getaways stretching in every direction.

How to get there: Enter Montrose and go to the town's main stoplight, which is the intersection of three major highways. Take Highway 90 west. A short way out of town the road splits and one artery appears to go straight ahead. Take the sharp left to stay on 90. After less than a mile, a sign quickly appears for Dave Wood Road. Take the road and go 11 miles, the last 3 miles on gravel, to the camp entrance on the left.

81. San Juan Bible Camp

14260 Road 39.9
Mancos, CO 81328
970-533-7622
www.sjbiblecamp.org

*S*olitude and activity meet at this rough-and-ready camp. Kids who attend in the summertime will plunge into an array of fun, muscle-stretching sports, while their spiritual lessons challenge them to remain centered on Jesus Christ. If they have not made such a commitment to Christ—and those kids are welcome here, too—they will be encouraged to do so while they are here. Spiritual lessons are mixed and sweetened with rousing activities that promote cooperative skills. Challenge courses and playing fields create cheerful spaces on the quiet meadows. An array of other activities, from wilderness backpacking to skiing and Ping-Pong, is also there for the taking.

Adults and church groups, which attend in the off-season, will find plenty of wandering space among sun-dappled meadows and forestland. They supply their own programs, which are expected to be Bible and

Christian oriented. The camp also welcomes family reunions. "Be sure and tell people this isn't a resort," says Paul Young, who in 2000 was in his fourth year of running the camp with his wife, Connie. What he means is that the accommodations are rustic, not elegant. The central lodge is a cozy dining hall off the industrial-sized kitchen. Upstairs is a warren of dormitory-style bedrooms that sleep a half-dozen or more. Scattered around the camp are bunk-style cabins for the more hardy.

The 20 acres are put to good use in a succession of naturally kept prairies flanked by towering ponderosa pines. Just within eyesight is a pretty meadow, which holds part of Colorado's history: the path for narrow-gauge trains that ran between 1880 and 1950. In another meadow kids take part in a "relay race" that confronts them with mind-bending tasks such as moving a whole team across a suspended board without falling off. The games are designed to help them develop communication, leadership, and problem-solving skills.

Fort Faith, the outdoor chapel where everyone gathers for prayer and a last-night fun and prayer fest, is a campfire area encircled by a high, Davy Crockett–style log enclosure: sturdy and rustic, just like the camp.

Location: About 30 miles west of Durango in the La Plata Range.

Description: An activities-oriented, interdenominational Christian camp.

Guest Profile: Youth camps in summer; adults, family reunions, marriage retreats, and individuals welcome other times.

Spiritual Experience: Lots of solitude in the lovely, forested prairie. Groups are expected to run Biblically oriented programs.

How to get there: Take Highway 160 west from Durango toward Cortez. Go 29 miles to Mancos, and take Highway 184 north 2.5 miles. Start slowing down—it's easy to miss the small sign indicating Highway 40. Turn right onto this gravel road and go 2.6 miles to a yellow cattle guard. Take the sharp left. Watch closely for the second right, marked as Road 39.9. The camp is half a mile down on the right, between two low stone pillars.

82. Sonlight Christian Camp

P.O. Box 536
Pagosa Springs, CO 81147
970-264-4379
www.sonlightcamp.org

*G*uests are greeted at the door of Sonlight with homemade cookies, fresh out of the oven. Now *that's* a retreat experience.

As it happens, this camp caters exclusively to a cookie-loving population: boys and girls from third to twelfth grades. This popular, nonprofit Christian camp, often booked months in advance, accommodates 64 guests, who spread out in a resort-quality campus area deep in the forests of the San Juan Range. Guests have a choice of five cabins and a main lodge that boasts a multileveled deck with comfy Adirondack chairs overlooking a lovely campus green. Volleyball nets, seesaws, and picnic tables complete the sense that this woodsy haven is going to be fun. There's also a game room with a pool table, TV, and VCR.

The camp began in 1979 as a Christian backpacking wilderness experience led by Winston Marugg, who with his wife, Mary, still directs the camp and, yes, still leads the backpacking forays. The camp offers skiing programs in winter and spring. A spiritual mission surrounds it all. Groups supply their own programs and leadership, which must have a

Christian, though nondenominational, thrust. (After all, in one word, the camp's name is a dual reference to Jesus as Son of God and Light of the World.)

The camp is also home to elk, deer, wild turkeys, and an aviary's worth of lovely birds. At certain times of the year the air is thick with hummingbirds, blue jays, and finches. Guests are asked to enjoy nature's own endless stream of local guests and leave their pets at home.

Except for one month during the summer, Sonlight's role is solely as operator of the facility and chief hospitality provider. Those with a history at the camp get first shot at reserving space the following year.

Year round, Sonlight is in charge of the down-home hospitality. That includes supplying all the food, which, along with the endless supply of cookies, is homemade. Guests are encouraged to wander into the kitchen to chat. The Maruggs foster the sense of home away from home, says assistant director Beth Windsor: "It's really a haven for people to come to. When we meet them in the parking lot and say, 'Welcome home,' they have tears in their eyes."

Only one group is booked at a time, to give a better retreat experience. That means the group has to guarantee payment for at least 35 to 45 guests, depending on the season.

Location: 7.5 miles from Pagosa Springs.

Description: An activities-oriented camp that seeks to "build self-esteem, create community, and develop respect for others and the environment" in a Christian setting.

Guest Profile: Primarily for youth, with some adult groups. Previous groups get first shot at the next year's reservations.

Spiritual Experience: A high-activity camp with a separate backpacking program for high school age youth. The property itself has 3 miles of trails, ensuring lots of room for solitude.

How to get there: From Pagosa Springs' busy main street (Highway 160), go north on Fifth Street. Go slow: Fifth splits in two almost immediately. Veer left. The equivalent of a few blocks away, look for another split. Veer right onto Four Mile Road (County Road 400). Narrow but initially paved, this is a lovely, winding path through forest and meadow that becomes groomed gravel. Drive 5.5 miles. Look for a "Sonlight Place" sign, and turn left. You have about 1.5 miles to go, through a stone gate entrance. Turn left into the parking lot. A cheery sign reads, "We Knew You'd Make It."

83. Spes in Deo Franciscan Family Retreat Center

21661 Highway 550
Montrose, CO 81401-8713
970-249-3526
www.spesindeoretreat.com

Photo courtesy of Spes in Deo Franciscan Family Retreat Center

*D*irector Joyce Martin calls this a "quiet place of renewal." The Latin name, Spes in Deo, means "Hope in God." Martin and her husband, Peter, bought these eight acres of God's country in 1978. They prefer very small groups of "one or two—not too many at a time," she says. Martin is a Secular Franciscan—that is, a member of a Catholic group of laypeople who follow the ways (or "rule") of St. Francis of Assisi in their daily lives. Prayer, modest living, and hospitality mark their path.

Guests come here to be alone on "private retreat," to meditate while strolling the peach and apple orchards of this green valley. Catholics will appreciate the small chapel, which contains the Blessed Sacrament. Guests may also take advantage of Martin's spiritual direction certification from a Benedictine abbey in Pecos, New Mexico. She incorporates classic Christian philosophy with the Carl Jung–inspired techniques of dreamwork and religious symbolism. She also teaches centering prayer, the technique developed in part by Rev. Thomas Keating at St. Benedict's Monastery near Snowmass (see page 221). Martin is an artist who, back in the 1970s, created one of the first paintings of a "smiling Christ." Her philosophy emphasizes "the Christ-essence of light, love, and laughter." Her daughter, MaryJoy Martin, is an author and artist who helps run the retreat house.

Guests enjoy a unique treat when Martin takes them to meditate in the hot springs in Ouray, 27 miles away. She likes to tell the story of one religious brother (monk) who was skeptical about the idea of meditating there. Martin said she would teach him. But at first sight of the stunning springs he broke out into a spontaneous prayer-form: "God, this is beautiful!" to which Martin replied, "See, I don't even have to teach you."

By the way, there's another moral to this story: Be sure to bring a bathing suit.

Location: About 9 miles south of Montrose.

Description: A small, home-style retreat center, set under a geodesic dome, catering to individuals and small groups.

Guest Profile: Open to people of any denomination. Reservations a must.

Spiritual Experience: Solitude is the norm, with spiritual direction available from the director. She also offers direction in the use of centering prayer, dreamwork, and "creative discovery" in fine arts, gardening, and music.

How to get there: From Montrose, take Highway 550 south about 9 miles. Keep your eyes peeled for the center, which will be to the west. It's marked by two geodesic domes. Look for the blue entrance sign.

84. Spirit Rest Retreat and Holistic Health Center

P.O. Box 1916
Pagosa Springs, CO 81147
970-264-2573
www.spiritrest.com

*I*f you don't already believe in feng shui, you may become a convert the moment you see this lovely pine lodge set high on a hill. The Oriental theory which suggests that the creation of spatial harmony impacts one's interior well-being seems to permeate these 20 acres of winding pathways and meditative shrines. That goes, too, for the renovated lodge, with its guesthouse-quality bedrooms, a sunny kitchen/eating area, and a living room dominated by a 25-foot-high stone fireplace. It offers the promise of cozy, hot chocolate get-togethers with other guests whenever one's solitude time is done.

Owner Josie Sifft, a sports psychologist who in her youth considered joining a cloistered monastery, has used her instinct for contemplative solitude to create a reverent, tree-dappled haven for people of many religious traditions. Whereas in some hands such diversity seems forced or artificial, here every space seems constructed with respect and reverence. One lovely renovation is a small, light-strewn sitting room/greenhouse that looks onto the grounds. Many guests find it ideal for creative pursuits such as landscape painting. There is an area for massage therapy and a basement conference room area, which is also used for yoga classes and guided retreats.

Location: About 3 miles from Pagosa Springs.

Description: A year-round retreat experience designed to help individuals and small groups "reconnect with Spirit/Nature/God in a peaceful mountain setting."

Guest Profile: All welcome who love solitude.

Spiritual Experience: Solitude, and private space, are respected here. There are serious getaway and alone places—compliments of both the owner and Mother Nature—as well as a lodge for reconnecting with fellow guests.

How to get there: From Pagosa Springs' busy main street (Highway 160), go north on Fifth Street. Go slow: Fifth splits in two almost immediately. Veer left. The equivalent of a few blocks away, look for another split. Veer right onto Four Mile Road (County Road 400). Narrow but initially paved, this is a lovely, winding path through forest and meadow. Go 3.2 miles; the last part is groomed gravel. Watch closely for the center's sign on your right.

In quiet arbors are benches and classically rendered statues dedicated to St. Francis of Assisi and the Blessed Virgin Mary. Down another path is an arbor dedicated to Buddha, whose statue is surrounded by colorful prayer flags. High on a cliff top (accessible by a hearty climb) is a shrine with tepee and medicine wheel dedicated to Native American culture. Guests may also sign up for vision quest—an intense, Lakota-inspired time of solitude and food/water deprivation said to bring on mystical experiences.

Guests will likely find their own favorite spots: Perhaps the geodesic-domed greenhouse? Or the labyrinth, a pathway maze of ankle-high stones? When done thoughtfully, walking a labyrinth—an ancient practice—is said to help one sort through life's entanglements.

For many, the center's tour de force will be the small, igloo-shaped hermitage for one. It costs the same to stay here as at the lodge, and the owner will even bus your meals. This cozy getaway, tucked into the woods, has a skylight and screened sides, which peel back to let in both sunlight and moonlight. Sifft's instinct for winsome hominess is everywhere: The bed is dressed with a lovely quilt, and an antique-style desk rounds out the space. There's even a port-a-potty for the really solitude minded, but the lodge and its several bathrooms are accessible and just a brisk, five-minute walk away.

Some guests have become semipermanent residents. There are just a few hard-and-fast rules: No kids, no pets, no drugs, and only guests who can respect other people's space.

85. St. Benedict's Monastery

1012 Monastery Road
Snowmass, CO 81654-9399
970-927-3311

Sometimes scenery alone can do the heavy lifting for the soul. Here you may find meditation and prayer come more easily as you drink in the lovely scene before you: A wide meadow dotted with cows stretches off to a ring of peaks, dominated by the elegant lines of Mt. Sopris, 12,953 feet high.

This huge acreage, which includes tiny, two-person hermitages as well as a resort-quality lodge and main monastery, has become enormously popular. Good luck making a reservation, as they're booked many months ahead. If you do find a place, you'll take part in a unique experience living on grounds with monks of the Cistercian Order of the Strict Observance. The monks of that heavy handle are better known as Trappists, the order made famous by the late author, essayist, poet, and activist monk, Thomas Merton, who lived at the monastery in Kentucky. The order came to Colorado in 1956.

Here, guests can pray during scheduled times alongside monks, who spend much of their day in silence and contemplation. Day guests are welcome to come for Sunday Mass and walk the lovely grounds dotted by aspen groves. Other weekly liturgies are available, but you should call for times.

Location: Snowmass, 10 miles from Aspen.

Description: A monastery for Benedictine monks that welcomes retreat guests.

Guest Profile: All welcome.

Spiritual Experience: Solitude beckons under the gaze of towering Mt. Sopris.

How to get there: On Highway 82 between Glenwood Springs and Aspen, look for a Conoco station at a stoplight intersection 10 miles west of the Aspen airport or—coming from the direction of Glenwood Springs—3 miles east of the main stoplight in Basalt. At that intersection, take the road that goes up the hill (left from Aspen, right from Glenwood Springs). Note: The monastery's directions call it Snowmass Creek Road but you may see it marked as Lower River Road. They are one and the same. Go up the hill about 1.75 miles and look for a "T" intersection, which is Capital Creek Road. Turn right. Go about 3.5 miles, and look for the monastery sign.

86. Tara Mandala Retreat Center

P.O. Box 3040
(903 San Juan Street)
Pagosa Springs, CO 81147
970-264-6177
Fax: 970-264-6169
www.taramandala.com

*W*ild, overgrown, understated: This Tibetan Buddhist retreat center makes no bones about the state of its sprawling acreage deep in the San Juan Forest. By the same token, the office, in the heart of Pagosa Springs 15 miles away, is focused and well organized. Taking them together, guests can experience both an untrammeled meditative experience and one that links them with Buddhism's most respected leaders worldwide, who come here to give retreats and seminars.

The office is where each guest must begin the journey, and it's the only place to get directions to the retreat center. It's the nerve center for an international enterprise that embraces an annual newsletter, a mail-order catalog, an educational institute, and scholarship programs as well as the sponsorship of world-renowned Tibetan teachers. (Besides its links with other Tibetan Buddhists worldwide, Tara Mandala has a companion center, Yeshe Korlo, in Crestone. Call Tara Mandala for more information.) Armed with a map, guests make their way from the office to the retreat grounds, mostly over dirt road through vast meadowlands and forests studded by ponderosa pine.

During summer 2000, the wilderness area hosted a month-long retreat with Adzom Parlo Rinpoche, a revered teacher in the Dzog Chen tradition. But activities and special teaching guests abound, year round. There is also a hermitage cabin available for rental.

The setting is rough-hewn wilderness. Guests sleep in tents and lean-tos scattered over a wide area, some barely visible through the network of scrub pines and piñons. Many guests have domesticated their makeshift villages with "porches" of plastic lawn chairs and cooking stoves, giving things a rakishly festive air.

Location: About 15 miles from Pagosa Springs.

Description: A retreat center and organization dedicated to promoting teachings of innate wisdom, specifically in the Tibetan Buddhist tradition.

Guest Profile: Anyone interested in learning about Tibetan Buddhist traditions.

Spiritual Experience: Guests may seek deep solitude in this natural wilderness area and participate in an array of conference and meditation groups.

How to get there: In Pagosa Springs, take Eighth Street south from the town's main street. Go 5 blocks to Apache. Turn right. The street becomes Trujillo Road (County Road 600), winds around, and turns to gravel. When you've gone 11 miles, look for a vivid red barn on your left. Take the Forest Service road right, and go 3.8 miles. You'll begin to see Buddhist prayer flags and narrow drive-paths. Take the second left (the first left will probably also get you to the driveway). Go slow, because the area is overgrown and crisscrossed with tents and meditating Buddhists.

Cooking is outdoors. So is the serious business of retreat work—including talks, discussion groups, and meditation. Small circles of guests and teachers, seated on folding chairs, dot the landscape.

A highlight of the new millennium was the consecration of the "stupa," or prayer altar, which dominates one of the wilderness clearings. Tara Mandala also hopes to develop a Drub-dra, or year-round meditation center, to accommodate 21 people, and a home for up to 10 elders who wish to live on the grounds permanently.

87. Treasure Mountain Bible Camp

500 East Park Street
Marble, CO 81623
970-963-1798

$\mathcal{L}$ ocated just beyond the town of Marble, with its bed-and-breakfasts and freshly painted Victorians, this cozy Bible camp is tucked into a steep-walled gorge near the Maroon Bells Wilderness Area. The camp aims to attract a certain kind of guest: Bible-believing and centered on Jesus Christ. Anyone else would likely find their week here a waste of time, says the director.

Indeed, the camp's layout is so intimate that guests surely need to be able to interact like family. As you enter the camp you're greeted by life-sized cutouts of pioneers and Indians, a theme that's carried out right down to the tomahawk-shaped door handles. Guests live in brightly colored, strong-sided tepees (not fabric), positioned a comfortable 25 paces or so apart. The central lodge is a sturdy log cabin.

The camp combines prayer, Bible study, and fun. Within sight of the main lodge and tepees, kids can plunge down a huge water slide into a pond or swing from seats hanging from massive, rough-hewn poles. There's a range of other activities, from canoeing to archery.

Location: About 40 miles south of Glenwood Springs.

Description: A rustic, activities-oriented camp for youth, families, couples, and singles.

Guest Profile: Christians with a strong belief in the Bible.

Spiritual Experience: Bible-oriented, with opportunities for spiritual getaways in the steep-gorged forest.

How to get there: From Carbondale, go south on Highway 133 until you just reach the start of McClure Pass. There you will see the left-turn sign for the town of Marble. (From the other direction, slow down as you descend McClure; the sign comes up quickly.) You are now 8 miles down a dirt road from the camp. Drive through Marble. The final leg is up a steep 2-mile gravel road along a cliff. (The famed Marble Quarry, a favorite tourist attraction, lies a mile or two beyond the camp.)

88. Voice of Wilderness

11003 Meadow Rue
The Woodlands, TX 77380
281-367-8842
E-mail: chet@voiceofwilderness.org

*A*h, wilderness. This Christian backcountry experience says what it means. The retreat zigzags so far off the roadway into the San Juans, by more than 15 miles, that the Russells don't even let guests drive there themselves. They go meet them.

Since 1973, the Russells have given their guests a one-week backpacking experience that combines physical, educational, and spiritual values. Everything they do is based on discipline, and their 35 acres of

Location: San Juan National Forest near Pagosa Springs.

Description: A wilderness experience for soul and body.

Guest Profile: Hardy folks willing to take on "the discipline of isolation."

Spiritual Experience: Solitude, activity, and disciplined prayer times.

How to get there: Have the Russells meet you.

rough-hewn living is designed to stiffen the spine as it stretches the soul. There's room for 15 to sleep in the small lodge, which boasts not only a full kitchen but a 1,000-volume library. Each week is different. Groups include families, singles, couples, and special "theme" weeks such as fathers with their sons. Depending on the skills of the group, some of the backpacking treks are rated high in difficulty.

Everyone should arrive with a small Bible.

The first night out, guests are led to a rock in a huge meadow and cautioned not to look back. Once they arrive, the Russells spring the surprise: a wow-of-a-vista that sets the tone for a week of living in God's country.

Every day, guests are asked to spend at least half an hour alone to pray and absorb nature, which they call "the discipline of isolation." By the end of the week, the Russells hope their guests have grown in four basic virtues: commitment, obedience, perseverance, and service. This wilderness experience also emphasizes caring for the environment, no-trace camping, erasing fire scars, and survival skills.

During the off-season, the Russells head home to Texas but leave the retreat in other hands for reunions, weddings, and family get-togethers. Hunters would love to come, too, says the couple, but that isn't quite in the spirit of the place.

89. Whitewater Community

8250 Kannah Creek Road (attn: Sister Anne Brost or Sister Mary Glenn)
Whitewater, CO 81527
970-241-3847

Whitewater Community began in 1971 when three members of the Visitation Order of nuns came to Colorado to establish a place where they could return to a more simple life of poverty and monasticism. Less than a decade later, the women were independent of the order and established as a spiritual community in the Catholic Diocese of Pueblo. The community maintains the simple lifestyle and invites others to join them, on a permanent or temporary basis.

Groups and individuals are welcome. Guests may choose to come for a one-day "getaway" or stay longer and immerse themselves in the life of the community. Mornings are devoted to silent prayer, study, and jogging. Afternoons may be devoted to housework, retreat preparation, or activities such as weaving. The sisters offer spiritual direction and structured retreats, or guests may fashion their own retreat experience.

The sisters continue to gather for what's been known for centuries in the Catholic Church as the "Liturgy of the Hours." Guests are welcome to join them for those daily recitations of prayers and hymns, which take place in the small chapel. The sisters are active in local parishes and attend workshops on contemporary spirituality.

Four private rooms are available to guests in the rustic farmhouse. A simple log cabin is also available on the 100-acre grounds for a more solitary experience.

Location: About 25 miles southeast of Grand Junction.

Description: A year-round retreat center run by a group of Catholic women dedicated to prayer, simplicity of life, and hospitality.

Guest Profile: Groups and individuals.

Spiritual Experience: Dedicated to small community living, solitude, and a simple lifestyle.

How to get there: The community prefers to give directions only to those they have spoken with and accepted for a retreat experience.

Sacred Places

90. Hovenweep National Monument

Stand here, and then *try* to call these ruins.

Broken yet dignified, the solitary towers and cliff dwellings of Mesa Verde National Park (see page 231) and Hovenweep National Monument rise as silent monuments to a vanished age. The word "ruins" hardly seems fitting to describe the wealth of artifacts, spiritual symbolism, artwork, and the enduring *presence* that the ancient Puebloans left for posterity 700 years ago. Today, visitors attuned to the spiritual things of life will come away enlightened and touched by what they find here.

These mysterious cliff dwellings and towers are the premier destinations for anyone hoping to experience the aura of ancient Puebloan cultures. Situated 50 miles west of Mesa Verde—the huge national park between Durango and Cortez in the southwest corner of Colorado—Hovenweep Monument is also under the park's custodial wing.

Civilizations thrived here from A.D. 500 to 1300. Then what happened? The name Hovenweep—an Indian word meaning "the deserted valley"—seems to speak with a mysterious poignancy to that point. Some believe a local 20-year drought that began in 1276 began to drive the tribes away. What they left behind was graceful stone dwellings that may have been used for all sorts of functions: defensive positions, storage areas, homes, religious sites, or celestial observation points. Ancient Puebloans carried out ceremonies in underground chambers, or kivas. "These are all sacred sites," says David Grant Noble, a writer and student of archaeological sites. "Descendants of these people considered their ancestral homes to be sacred places—their ancestors are buried there and the spirits of their ancestors are still there."

To get to Hovenweep from Cortez, take Highway 666 north. After 19 miles, in the town of Pleasant View turn left onto dirt County Road CC. Drive 5.5 miles and turn left (south) on County Road 10. Go another 21.5 miles to the park. Thinking they're lost, "lots of people turn around and go back to Cortez," says park ranger David Tam. "They've got to have faith." For ye of little faith, he offers another route, on a mostly-paved road for about 40 miles: Take Highway 666 south 2.5 miles, and when you see the sign for the Cortez airport, turn right onto the service road that passes the airport. Stay on this road, County Road G along McElmo Canyon—it will take you straight to Hovenweep. The roads here are old farming routes that crisscross and meander, so stay alert for the "Hovenweep" signs that nudge you in the right direction. For more information, call the monument office at 970-562-4282.

91. Mesa Verde National Park

"Twenty-four [tribal] nations consider this a sacred religious place— a place where their ancestors lived and where spirits reside," says Will Morris, spokesman for Mesa Verde. Nor is it a site that speaks only to the past: Hopi elders, looking at ancient petroglyph panels, have recognized their own modern-day symbols. Various tribes use several springs in the area for religious and cultural ceremonies. When those rites are scheduled, the immediate area is sometimes closed to the public.

Visitors have their own access to history. The park's goal "is to convey to visitors a direct connection to a living past," Morris says. An excellent place to begin your tour is the Chapin Mesa Archeological Museum. "It's the best place for artifacts. Sandals, woven cotton cloth, pottery, jewelry—it's just amazing to get the sense of human beings creating these beautiful and functional things," says Morris. Be sure to see Spruce Tree House, the best-preserved cliff dwelling at the park, open year-round. The largest is Cliff Palace, with 151 rooms, but it's virtually inaccessible during winter.

To get to Mesa Verde, take Highway 160 west from Durango about 36 miles and look for the clearly marked signs on the highway. For more information, call 970-529-4465.

Other Spiritual Destinations

Twin Peaks Bible Camp
P.O. Box 907, Grand Junction, CO 81502; 970-487-3891
"The beautiful Rocky Mountains is our setting for biblical teaching." Located in Grand Mesa National Forest 7 miles south of Collbran (east of Grand Junction), this year-round camp for couples, youth, and families offers special outreach to senior citizens. From I-70, take Exit 49 for the town of Mesa, and drive on Highways 65 and 330 to Collbran, where you'll turn right for the 7 miles to the camp.

Twin Peaks Bible Camp near Grand Mesa National Forest is a summer camp and retreat providing Biblical training and spiritual outreach.

Region Seven:
Western Slope North and Central

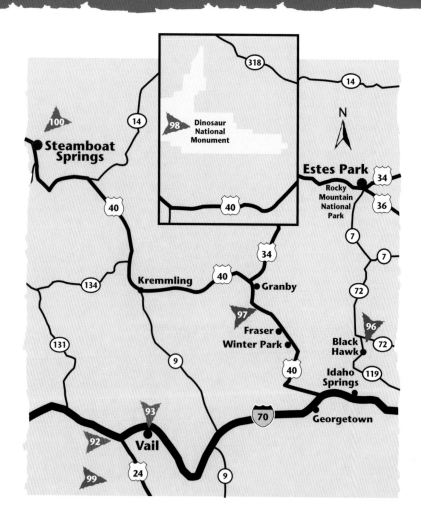

318

14

100

14

98 Dinosaur National Monument

N

Steamboat Springs

40

40

US 34

Estes Park

Rocky Mountain National Park

US 36

34

40

Kremmling

40

Granby

7

7

134

97

72

131

Fraser
Winter Park

96

Black Hawk

72

9

40

Idaho Springs

119

93

70

Georgetown

92

Vail

99

24

9

*I*n this vast chunk of Colorado, your spiritual destinations take in everything from two sweet chapel stops to an entire mountain. The premier ski resorts of Vail and Beaver Creek are synonymous with highbred leisure, but they also are home to a pair of interfaith sanctuaries that offer visitors small-town charm in a handsome setting. Meanwhile, those with adventure in their hearts may opt for an unusual pilgrimage to another Vail site, Mount of the Holy Cross, memorialized for a century in paintings and photographs.

To the north is one of the largest spiritual spots in the state: Snow Mountain Ranch, a veritable town's worth of activities and spiritual getaways. And snuggled against metro Denver's own Fourteener, Mt. Evans, are two very different retreat possibilities. One is run by a Reform Jewish congregation, the other by a Christian couple who say they plunged into retirement only to find that God had more for them to do.

Sanctuaries

92. The Chapel at Beaver Creek

P.O. Box 1146
Avon, CO 81620
970-845-9449

93. Vail Interfaith Chapel

P.O. Box 3712
Vail, CO 81658
970-476-3347
Vail Religious Foundation and Beaver Creek Religious Foundation
970-524-7342

Location: In the heart of Colorado's premier resort and ski country.

Description: "Working" chapels that hold regular church and synagogue services for tourists and locals.

Guest Profile: All welcome. Both are extremely popular for weddings, bar and bat mitzvahs, and other spiritual celebrations; also open for programs such as Alcoholics Anonymous and AIDS awareness.

Spiritual Experience: An inspiring mountain setting for worship or reflection.

How to get there: Vail chapel: From I-70, take Exit 176, the middle of the three Vail exits. Go through the European-style roundabout and continue straight ahead on Vail Road into town. Drive the equivalent of a block or so, and you'll see the chapel on the right. Parking is at a premium, but there is a relatively spacious lot behind the chapel. **Beaver Creek chapel:** From I-70, take Exit 167, the Beaver Creek/Avon exit (west of the westernmost Vail exit). Follow the road all the way through Avon carefully—traffic is heavy and the intersections can get confusing. At the entrance to Beaver Creek, you'll come upon a guard's gate. Stop and get a pass to the chapel. Wind up the hill for a few miles, almost to the top. Keep an eye out for the classic-looking stone chapel, on your left.

Opposite: The Chapel at Beaver Creek (shown here) and Vail Interfaith Chapel minister have a variety of interdenominational services.

*I*f you were around when Vail was a sheep pasture, you've been around awhile. For most, Vail is simply one of the world's great resorts and premier ski destinations.

But it was in those rural pasturelands way back in the early 1960s that the Vail Religious Foundation planted the seeds for the Vail and Beaver Creek interfaith chapels. Thanks to the long-ago foresight of a half-dozen church denominations, you can pause to pray and meditate far from—but not too far from—the glittering life on the slopes and in the exclusive shops of Vail and its sister city up the road, Beaver Creek. Both chapels are open daily.

Other resorts may have chapels, but these two are notable for the strong cooperative effort of these Christian congregations and one Jewish community. What makes them more unusual in the resort world is that these are not just tourist destinations but serious places of worship for the townsfolk. The newly-renovated Vail chapel, headquarters for the interfaith foundation, is a picture-perfect ski chalet in the heart of the town. Its success in attracting worshipers for both regular services and special holidays and events encouraged the foundation to build another chapel in Beaver Creek. Even in those days, land was scarce and many denominations knew they could never afford, or find, a place to put their churches.

In the late 1960s, the Lutheran Church in America sent Pastor Don Simonton to plant a church in Vail. What started as an experiment proved to be a beloved part of the community. So in 1980 Simonton was asked to assist in finding a Beaver Creek site that would pass the required environmental impact statement. The site he found was irresistible.

Simonton was on horseback, scouting sites high on the Beaver Creek mountainside, when he spied a grove of trees that looked unusual compared to the rest. He took a leaf sample and found it was the same fragrant poplar that the pioneers had called "the balm of Gilead," from the Bible. Only half kidding, Simonton told Beaver Creek developers that he had found the perfect site for the companion chapel—right in a grove of poplars made famous by Scripture. As it turned out, the site did indeed prove to fit all the development criteria, and so it became home to the chapel. Today, a remnant of the poplar grove is clustered about the handsome stone chapel, and the "balm of Gilead" theme is carried throughout in golden leaves sculptured on doorways and chandeliers. The interior is a mellow shade of vanilla gold, with greenery and rich wooden beams creating a soul-soothing atmosphere.

Although located in two of America's wealthiest havens, the chapels take their social responsibility seriously. They open their doors to provide havens to transients and snowbound strangers with nowhere to go. Of course, they can't help also being the center of life for a flock that has included famous folks. The funeral of the founder of the Head ski company was held in the Vail chapel, and former President Gerald Ford has served on the interfaith chapel board and been among the worshipers at Beaver Creek chapel on Christmas Eve.

Retreats

94. Camp Shwayder

c/o Congregation Emanuel
51 Grape Street
Denver, CO 80220
303-388-4013
Fax: 303-388-6328
www.shwayder.com

*A*fter all the horseback riding, rope courses, and hiking is done, this camp offers what may be an unusual sight on a backcountry weekend: young people all dressed up in nice khakis and dresses. If it's Friday, this must be kabalat shabbat: The traditional singing and parade to celebrate the Sabbath (shabbat), which begins at sundown. At Camp Shwayder, the mix of fun and heritage draws young people from across the country.

Camp Shwayder is named for its benefactor, Maurice Shwayder, a member of Congregation Emanuel who donated the property back in the 1940s. Not only is Congregation Emanuel the oldest Jewish congregation in Colorado, but Camp Shwayder is one of the oldest Reform Jewish camps in the United States.

The camp is set on a rustic hillside in deep forest. Guests in 2000 found new cabins with bunk beds and a new dining hall. The meals are kosher-style, meaning no pork or shellfish and all meat and dairy foods are served

Location: In the heart of Arapaho National Forest, 9 miles from Idaho Springs.

Description: A rustic camp for youth and families in the Reform Jewish tradition.

Guest Profile: Youth ages 8 to 16 (third through tenth grades) during summer. Adult and family retreat time available mid-August to mid-September.

Spiritual Experience: Dedicated to promoting Jewish values and lifestyles and providing an atmosphere for positive Jewish living.

How to get there: Take I-70 west to Idaho Springs. Take the highway's second Interstate exit, 240, for Highway 103, also marked as the road to Mt. Evans. Drive 9 miles, and look for the camp's green gate on the right. (See map on p. 98.)

Young campers studying the Torah at Camp Shwayder. Photo courtesy of Rabbi Mark Covitz.

separately. A kosher kitchen follows strict rules regarding food preparation. (For another camp with a kosher kitchen, see the JCC Ranch on page 138.)

During the day, the camp bristles with activities, including fine arts, drama, music, and art programs. A rabbi serves as camp director, and there is also time for study of the Torah and the Jewish heritage. As summer winds down, the camp hosts adult retreat groups in the reform Jewish tradition.

95. Christian Prayer Retreat House

8810 State Highway 103
Idaho Springs, CO 80452
303-567-4601

Location: About 9 miles from Idaho Springs.

Description: "We seek to serve disciples of Jesus Christ with a safe, beautiful, and warmly hospitable place of retreat for their prayer purposes."

Guest Profile: Christians seeking solitude for a few hours or days.

Spiritual Experience: Solitude is the backbone of the house, with spiritual guidance available upon request.

How to get there: Follow I-70 west to Idaho Springs and the town's second Interstate exit, 240 (Highway 103 and the route to Mt. Evans). Drive 8.8 miles on the winding mountain road to the retreat house, which is on your right and well marked with a sign and parking turnout adjacent to the roadway. (See map on p. 98.)

"Lord, what should we be doing for you?" When Jan Bauer asked the question, she was on her Hawaiian balcony overlooking a fragrant sea of tropical flowers. Most folks would have been content to leave things just as they were, thank you very much. But Bauer, a retired schoolteacher, and her husband, George, a retired airline pilot, felt a longing to rock their boat for God.

Rock it, they did. The couple left their island paradise for the close embrace of the Rocky Mountains and Arapaho National Forest, 9,500 feet higher than the limpid beaches of Hawaii. Jan became an ordained Presbyterian minister. Their "adventure in faith," as she calls it, was beginning to take shape. Together, the couple sought out experts, both Catholic and Protestant, to instruct them in the long Christian heritage of retreats.

The result is a serene, Swiss-style chalet nestled beside a tumbling brook, as peaceful inside as out. On the site of a century-old lodge the Bauers have fashioned a serious retreat experience in surroundings of elegant simplicity.

First of all, guests may sense that this isn't a retreat house as much as a retreat home. Built in 1995, the chalet has 10 bedrooms—seven upstairs, three down—set along carpeted hallways and decorated with furniture from

George's antique collecting days. Most rooms have a private sink, with gleaming modern bathrooms across the hall. A striking Japanese wall treatment, picked up in George's travels, adds to the sense of meditative harmony. A small prayer closet—literally a closet—is available for personal prayer. A den/lounge area is dressed in soothing cream colors accented with an Oriental carpet and the cozy glow of a woodstove.

All the surroundings are designed to encourage quiet and reflection. The Bauers have even added sound suppression curtains so that individual retreatants may have more private dining in the pleasantly well-turned-out dining hall, where they serve three meals daily. Even groups are encouraged to use the dining experience as a time for quiet prayer. For guests who have not been exposed to the ancient Christian practice of silent retreats, Jan promises them: "This is going to be an adventure in your spiritual life."

An ordained minister, Jan offers Christian worship services daily and Sunday upon request. She's also available for individual and group retreat direction. Of course, guests may follow their own path to solitude. The chapel, down a carpeted hallway, is a great place to begin. Peace radiates from the graceful sanctuary, with its tall open windows looking out onto the deep forests, and the cream walls decorated whimsically with wood rescued from the 1903 lodge. Even here, the Bauers have brought their own distinctively personal touch. The Bauers' son built the gleaming wood pulpit, while their daughter did the lovely quiltwork in the bedrooms.

Guests are encouraged to wander outdoors, too. For a truly solitary guest, there's a sturdy log hermitage about 30 paces from the chalet. Beyond, serious forest beckons. Wild and beautiful, the Arapaho National Forest has confounded even serious mountain hikers who come here on retreat. Although no guest has ever been lost for long, the Bauers keep close watch if their guests don't report back at dining times. When that happens, they literally call out their "prayer teams" to help bring home the lost. Those prayer partners—an actual group of serious Christian friends—have been in place since the Bauers came here. For any need, even a late-arriving guest, the Bauers call up the prayer teams to ask God for help. The couple credits their friends with the success of their spiritual enterprise from the beginning, when all they had was a plot of land and a call from God.

"We have 18 people who pray for us daily," says Jan. "The results are in the feedback we get from retreatants who say their time here has truly been filled with God's presence. When we came we were full of trepidation and not certain how the facility would be received—but God has graced us with beautiful people and more of an experience than we ever imagined."

96. Trinity Mountain Ranch

P.O. Box 597
Black Hawk, CO 80422-0597
303-642-3428

*T*his camp, a few miles from one of Colorado's gaming towns, specializes in diversity, says manager John Thilmont. To give you an idea of what he means: A recent gathering welcomed a group of Vietnamese Catholics who brought Buddhist friends. An environmentalist group from New Zealand came and went, "and took all the trash with them," he says. Next, a Baptist group fixed the water heater, which went on the fritz during a cold spell. "I will be indebted to Baptists forever," says Thilmont.

The lodge sleeps 53 in bunk beds. There are some single rooms too, mostly for retreat masters. The surroundings include 70 acres and a beautiful view of Indian Peaks. There's a baseball diamond dubbed (what else?) "The Field of Dreams." The remote area "appeals to many people who like their privacy," says Thilmont. Each group gets the camp to themselves, which adds to the seclusion and sense of purpose.

Location: 8 miles from Black Hawk.

Description: An interdenominational retreat center for groups of 30 or more.

Guest Profile: All welcome.

Spiritual Experience: The remote area lends itself to solitude, but the camp is set up for group get-togethers.

How to get there: Go to Sixth Avenue in Golden and follow Highway 6 west to the intersection with Highway 119 (marked Black Hawk/Central City). Take 119 north through Black Hawk, continuing to the second entrance to Golden Gate State Park. (You're 10 yards away when you see highway marker 155.) Go right; the road is also marked as Gap. Drive the equivalent of a city block and look for another right. Turn there, go the equivalent of seven city blocks, and look for a "Fellowship Camp" sign. Turn left, continue six or seven blocks, and look for the "Trinity Mountain Ranch" sign.

97. YMCA of the Rockies/ Snow Mountain Ranch

Winter Park, CO 80482
970-887-2152
E-mail: info@ymcarockies.org
www.ymcarockies.org

*D*on't be confused: This isn't a small town, it just seems like one.
Roads meander through this lovely 5,100-acre complex, taking you to
some very interesting destinations, indeed. How many other retreat and
conference centers include a kidney dialysis building and a petting zoo?
Armed with the excellent map provided at the front desk, you should have
a wonderful time browsing your way through the miles of facilities. Among
them is the "Hidden Sanctuary," one of several secluded spiritual destinations
that make this center special.

Location: Highway 40 between the ski resorts of Silver Creek (5 miles north) and Winter Park (12 miles south).

Description: Like its sister center in Estes Park (see page 36), Snow Mountain Ranch is marketed with all the professional gloss of the YMCA organization. Welcoming and nondenominational, the YMCA's mission statement for both locations sums up everything by saying it "puts Christian principles into practice through programs, staff and facilities in an environment that builds healthy spirit, mind and body for all."

Guest Profile: All welcome. See YMCA/Estes Park Center, page 36, for more on rates and membership. Youth ages 8 to 16 can also sign on for a summer program at Camp Chief Ouray, located on the ranch grounds.

Spiritual Experience: Fashion your own experience from miles of secluded and paved roadways, a beautiful chapel, several secluded outdoor chapel sites, a "religious activity center," and a chaplain's office.

How to get there: From Denver, take I-70 west to Highway 40, the Granby turnoff. Snow Mountain Ranch is about 12 miles north of Winter Park. Look for the sign on your left. If you're coming from the north (in the vicinity of Estes Park), you may be able to take that heart-thumper, Highway 34 west. Just west of Estes Park this route becomes Trail Ridge Road, which soars up to 12,000 feet through Rocky Mountain National Park. (Due to year-round storms and snow, Trail Ridge is closed more months of the year than it's open.) Eventually, Highway 34 meets Highway 40 south. When you get to Granby you're 7 miles from the ranch. When you pass Silver Creek you have 5.4 miles to go. Look carefully for the sign on the right—it comes up fast, just around a small curve.

Somebody has certainly made Whispering Pines Chapel special. Some retreat-center chapels seem more like utilitarian meeting rooms stabbed in the front with a cross. The main chapel here, next to the administration lodge, says "church" in every detail—from its gleaming, burnished overhead beams and soft track lighting to the majestic red carpet leading to an altar. Bibles are on every chair, and nondenominational services are held every Sunday.

Like its sister center in Estes Park, Snow Mountain Ranch is loaded with activities, scenery, and overnight accommodations. Cross-country skiing is just one of the many activities available on these vast grounds, with major ski resorts, of course, just a few miles away.

The kidney dialysis center, by the way, is a special service that allows patients to plan a full vacation here without worrying about treatment. Its schedule, as of 2001, was dialysis

YMCA of the Rockies/Snow Mountain Ranch offers unique amenities, a youth camp, nondenominational services, and a number of chapels and outdoor chapel sites.

service on Mondays, Wednesdays, and Fridays, and closed the months of November through January. Be sure to call for details and possible schedule changes.

For those seeking a spiritual component, the sheer size and layout of the ranch offers its own unlimited ways to be secluded and prayerful. Be sure to seek out the Outdoor Chapel near Columbine Point, several miles from the administration building on a paved road. (Signage is excellent throughout the complex, so you should have no trouble finding things.) A brief, off-road hike of several hundred paces takes you to a very meditative spot. Appearing before you, in the middle of nowhere, is a homespun outdoor chapel consisting of tiers of rough wooden benches facing a large cross. Beyond, toothy crags jut into the sky, and may well pierce the soul.

Sacred Places

98. Dinosaur National Monument

*G*o west, dear visitor, and take in an ancient site: the history-laden Dinosaur National Monument, encompassing 210,000 acres splashed across Colorado and Utah. It made its mark in the early 20th century as one of the world's largest dinosaur fossil sites of the Jurassic period.

But now it's also known as an ancient neighborhood of Native American culture. The archaeological evidence goes back 9,000 years, says Rich Jehle, the monument's Yampa district interpreter. Most accessible are the rock-art sites, although they have varying levels of accessibility. To guard against vandalism, some sites are not disclosed. In any case, don't expect "big panels of art," says Jehle. Many of these petroglyphs, or rock carvings, "are subtle, but real nonetheless." Jehle also suggests visiting Cañon Pintado, on Highway 139 south of Rangely and Highway 64, to observe more rock art.

Then there's a collection of petroglyphs in Irish Canyon, about 10 miles outside the monument area, north of the monument's Gates of Lodore. This wilderness study area "is apparently a sacred area to Native Americans," says Richard Rhinehart, author of *Colorado Caves*. He cites the south entrance to the scenic canyon as a side road leading to petroglyphs decorating the boulders.

Among the Native American cultures that settled here were the so-called Fremont people, a band of seminomadic hunter-gatherers. They left a great mark throughout northwestern Colorado, much of it inside the monument area. Also referred to as the "Desert Archaic folk," they disappeared from the landscape about 600 years ago. However, they left behind echoes of their presence in about 300 sites in the area, according to David Grant Noble, author of *Ancient Colorado*. To glimpse something of their vanished presence, guests can still visit Mantle Cave, located within the monument along the Yampa River. Inside the cave, archaeologists found a 37-room food storage area—and something else.

A treasure of ceremonial items was cached away in what Noble describes as "a voluminous vaulted alcove." The most prized was a ceremonial headdress in near-perfect condition, a very rare find anywhere in North America. That magnificent headdress, composed of ermine, buckskin, and nearly 400 feathers, was sent for safekeeping to the University of Colorado Museum in Boulder.

Dinosaur National Monument is about 300 miles from Denver. That's the shorter route, using US Highway 40. If you take I-70 (cutting north from Rifle), you'll add about 75 miles to the trip. For more information, call the monument headquarters in Dinosaur at 970-374-3000. As for getting to Mantle Cave, Jehle suggests the river trip, an option offered by the monument staff. The route by car and foot is difficult on the steep and craggy landscape, which in some spots is about 1,000 feet above the cave. At one point, says Jehle, it even requires "tying a rope to a tree and doing a bat walk for about 30 or 40 feet."

99. Mount of the Holy Cross

Photo courtesy of John Fielder

*F*or how many millennia has the cross stood there? Today, visitors can still go on a guided pilgrimage, or one of their own, to this natural-made holy scene that has captured hearts since at least the 19th century.

A century ago, the graceful, crisscrossed gully outlined in snow and cut in the heart of this 14,005-foot peak was famous, second in tourist interest only to Pikes Peak. It became a national monument, and the stuff of obsession—but how ever does one get there, to see it up close?

In 1873, the renowned photographer William Henry Jackson hiked to the top of nearby Notch Mountain and captured the glory of this natural shrine. Its fame took off. By excursion train, horseback, and on foot, people came to this remote area of the Vail Valley. You can still come today on hikes that have lured even spry 80-year-olds. Although rockslides and time have somewhat smeared its perfect symmetry, the cross figure is still impressive. Counterintuitive as it is, the best time to absorb the scene is July: That's when just the right amount of snowmelt makes this natural-made Christian symbol, standing in its perpetual aerie, stand out at its best.

The Rev. Carl Walker, pastor of Mount of the Holy Cross Lutheran Church in Vail, leads organized hikes. Ever since 1976 his congregation has led trips up Notch Mountain at the end of July. The hikes are free but limited to 25 people. Walker's church leads special group retreats and small parties of folks who want to go at other times as well. Of course, you can also get there on your own. If you do, you will likely use the standard Forest Service map. That's a somewhat longer route than the one taken by the church, which uses an old pilgrimage trail map no longer available to the public.

The full-day pilgrimage begins at 7 a.m. and returns at 4 p.m. It's an 8-mile round trip capped by a worship service overlooking the Mount. It's a strenuous hike: While there are no dangerous "mountain climbing" exposures, you will gain more than 2,000 feet in altitude. Bad weather is common—lightning has chased pilgrims down more than once—so be prepared with good rain gear as well as plenty of water and a bag lunch. You needn't be a super athlete but should be in good shape. Remember that the Mount is just over 14,000 feet in elevation and the service is held at 12,500 feet—more than 2 miles high.

Pilgrims meet at the ranger station at Minturn at the junction of Highway 24 and I-70 (Exit 171). Everybody carpools to the Half Moon Campground, a 15-mile drive. To sign up, call Mount of the Holy Cross Lutheran Church at 970-476-6610. For more information about the Mount of the Holy Cross, call the Holy Cross Ranger District of White River National Forest at 970-827-5715.

100. Strawberry Park Hot Springs

*W*hat part of the land is not sacred? Over and over again, Native Americans have cautioned against setting aside "somewhere" as sacred. Every place has its meaning.

Nowhere is the cautionary note more useful than on the Western Slope. Everywhere, an archaeological trail of tools and pottery, rock art and petroglyphs, cliff dwellings and caves points to Colorado's vital Native American presence through the ages. For visitors who wish to honor the continent's indigenous cultures—and spiritual beliefs—Strawberry Park Hot Springs is a great choice if you're in northwestern Colorado.

Hot springs appear to have been places of retreat and meditation for centuries. Just 8 miles from the heart of the resort town of Steamboat Springs, Strawberry Park Hot Springs' pools of ancient bubbly have undergone several transformations, according to Deborah Frazier George, author of *Colorado's Hot Springs*. "Local lore claims the Ute Indians used the hot springs after battles with other tribes to heal body and soul," she writes. "The Utes believe now, as they did hundreds of years ago, that the vapors contained their creator's essence and soaking in the pool rejuvenated the soul."

In the 1870s the Utes suffered the outrages of being swept into government-imposed reservations—and lost access to one of their culture's most intimate natural retreat areas. Over the next century, Strawberry Park Hot Springs would be overtaken by a loutish subculture that used the area for boisterous parties and hanging out. Then, in 1982, George writes, a man named Don Johnson bought the property, cleaned it up, chased off the transients, and paid tribute to the springs by dressing them up with beautiful stone walls. The crisscrossing walls add an intimate, meditative coziness to the scene. And natural landscaping has restored the alpine setting to a state the Utes probably saw here for centuries—what its current owners refer to as "a natural Eden."

To get to Strawberry Park Hot Springs, head northeast on Seventh Street in Steamboat Springs through a residential neighborhood to Park Road. Go north (left) onto a dirt road about 8 miles. For more information, call 970-879-0342.

Other Spiritual Destinations

Euzoa Retreat Center

32305 RCR 38, Steamboat Springs, CO 80487; 970-879-0576: "Find rest in the grace of God in the majestic beauty of the Colorado Rockies." Specializing in singles, this is also a year-round center for youth, families, couples, and adults.

Opposite: The Chapel at Beaver Creek.

Appendix A

Glossary

Ashram: A hermitage or retreat center, used in the tradition of Eastern religions and sometimes specifically referring to a yoga center or school.

Blessed Sacrament: The repository for the consecrated hosts, which Catholics believe have been changed from bread into the real body of Jesus Christ. Usually given the central place of honor in a church or chapel in a tabernacle, it's the believer's main object of worship and meditation.

Centering prayer: A prayer method popularized by the writings of the Rev. Thomas Keating, a Benedictine priest based in Snowmass. The method seeks to develop contemplation by teaching the person praying to use a sacred word as a symbol of consent to God's presence and action within, and to repeat the word, as necessary, to keep the mind free of conscious thought.

Contemplative: One who uses silent meditation and solitude to remain as much as possible in the presence of God, or the Divine.

Directed retreat. See *Retreat*

Dreamwork: A method of dream interpretation inspired by the work of Carl Jung, the Swiss psychiatrist and founder of analytical psychology.

Feng shui: An ancient Chinese art of placement and its philosophy of creating a harmonious environment.

Jewish denominations: Commonly divided into Orthodox, Conservative, and Reform. The terms refer to various understandings of how best to follow ancient Jewish law, ranging from the original, strict meanings to more modern, relaxed interpretations.

Labyrinth: A meditation tool dating back 4,000 years, in which one follows a concentric series of circles designed to open the mind and spiritual awareness. The labyrinth is not a maze, where the intent is to confuse, but, rather, many revolutions of one path. Adherents say the practice helps in exercising both the left and right brain. Thus, the labyrinth is excellent for meditation purposes and problem solving, whether of the practical or spiritual variety.

Mandala assessment: A technique for identifying childhood issues and other psychological blocks through symbolic drawings. The *mandala*, a Tibetan Buddhist term, is a visual presentation of symmetrically arranged circles-within-circles used as a meditative technique.

Mantra: A formula or word with spiritual significance, used in Eastern religions for meditation, focus, relaxation, or deep rest.

Novice: A beginner in a religious order.

Private retreat. See *Retreat*

Reiki energy work: A natural healing technique, based on the application of "Universal Life Force Energy," begun in the late 1800s by Mikao Usui, a teacher in a Japanese boys' school who set out to learn how Jesus and Buddha healed people. Usui attracted apprentice-followers, who helped evolve Reiki into a system of hand placements and body work. To be authentic, the technique must be passed down directly from one Reiki master to another.

Retreat: A period of prayer and spiritual reflection conducted away from one's regular worldly life. During a *directed retreat,* a trained spiritual guide helps the individual reach deeper levels of understanding. During a *private retreat,* the individual marks out a personal time for disciplined spiritual renewal and follows it alone, usually in silence and solitude.

Rinpoche: A Buddhist title indicating "teacher." The title appears at the end of the person's name: Thus, the Buddhist leader Chogyam Trungpa is referred to as Chogyam Trungpa Rinpoche or, more familiarly, Trungpa Rinpoche.

Shaman ("shamanistic"): Practitioner of ancient "magico-religious phenomena" familiar to many native religions. The shaman achieves an ecstatic trance state, in which the soul of the shaman is believed to leave the body to ascend to the heavens or the underworld.

Shambhala: Related to the English transliteration "Shangri-La." In the Buddhist lexicon, the term traditionally refers to an enlightened, utopian society.

Stations of the Cross: An ancient Christian devotion that marks 14 "stations," or incidents, on Jesus Christ's death walk to Calvary.

Stupa: The term means "mound," but the edifice is usually an elegant, towering structure designed to represent the enlightened mind of Buddha, and thus the core essence of Buddhist teaching.

Taize worship: A specific form of interfaith worship developed by a group of spiritual companions in Taize, France, shortly after World War II. The worship was meant to unite Christians of different denominations into one, traditional service using Scripture readings, prayers, and the hymns of ancient Christianity, usually sung in Latin. The worship style has spread around the world.

Torah: The first five books of the Bible. The Torah's theme is the origin of life and the ways God directed the Jews to live their lives as His chosen people. The term sometimes refers to the whole body of Jewish teaching, literature, and laws.

Vedic: Referring to the Vedas, the sacred scriptures of ancient India. Believers trace the Vedic period back 10,000 years, marked by a system of deities and reincarnation. Historically it came before Hinduism, though many use *Hindu* and *Vedic* interchangeably.

Vision quest: An ancient Native American spiritual method, experienced in rigorous solitude and deprivation, that hones the inner consciousness. It's become popular among many spiritual seekers.

Yoga: A Sanskrit word meaning "union." The term commonly refers to the Hindu-based discipline for developing and integrating energy—and unity with the Divine—through breathing techniques and body exercises.

Appendix B

Recommended Reading and Websites

Reading

Benedict, James B. *Old Man Mountain: A Vision Quest Site in the Colorado High Country*. Boulder, Colo.: Johnson Publishing Co., 1985. Obtain copies via the publisher or by writing to: Center for Mountain Archaeology, 8297 Overland Road, Ward, CO 80481.

George, Deborah Frazier. *Colorado's Hot Springs*. Boulder, Colo.: Pruett Publishing Co., 2000.

Kucin, Lynda, ed. *Crestone: An Illustrated Guide to the Significant Attractions of the Crestone/Baca Area*. Crestone, Colo.: The Way Productions, 2000. The guide costs $10. Obtain copies by writing to: The Way Productions, P.O. Box 320, Crestone, CO 81131 (719-256-4401).

Martorano, Marilyn. "Culturally Peeled Ponderosa Pine Trees, Great Sand Dunes National Monument." *San Luis Valley Historian* 23:3 (1990).

McDonald, Marci. "The New Spirituality: Hanne Strong Gathers the Religions of the World in Colorado." *Maclean's*. October 10, 1994.

Noble, David Grant. *Ancient Colorado: An Archaeological Perspective*. Denver: Colorado Council of Professional Archaeologists, 2000. Obtain copies by writing to: Colorado Council of Professional Archaeologists, P.O. Box 40727, Denver, CO 80204-0727.

Noble, David Grant. *Ancient Ruins of the Southwest: An Archaeological Guide*. Flagstaff, Ariz.: Northland Publishing, 2000.

Rhinehart, Richard. *Colorado Caves*. Englewood, Colo.: Westcliffe Publishers, 2001.

Websites

Christian Camping International: www.cciusa.org

Crestone Business Association: www.crestone.org

National Park Service: www.nps.gov

For suggested links to Eastern religion websites: www.ashram.com

The road to Horn Creek Retreat near Westcliffe.

Index

NOTE: Citations followed by the letter "p" denote photos;
citations followed by the letter "m" denote maps.

About the Author

Jean Torkelson is the religion writer for the *Rocky Mountain News* in Denver, where her weekly column, "How Coloradans Worship," highlights people and their religious traditions in a style and format considered unique among the country's newspapers. During a career spent as an editorial page writer, general interest columnist, television reporter, and governor's aide, she's made time for retreats and visits to religious centers in Europe as well as in Colorado, Pennsylvania, and her native Upper Midwest.

About the Photographer

Bill Bonebrake has lived in Colorado most of his life and through his work as a nature photographer has acquired a vast knowledge of the state. He concentrates his photographic efforts in the Rocky Mountains and in the Four Corners region. His images appear in books including Westcliffe Publishers' *Colorado Campgrounds: The 100 Best and All the Rest*, *Santa Fe: Dancing Ground of the Sun*, and *Colorado's Scenic Ghost Towns*, as well as on greeting cards and postcards produced through JAMIT Publishing. Bill's work also gains international exposure through stock agencies.